Queen
The Illustrated Biography

Queen
The Illustrated Biography

TIM HILL

Trans
Atlantic
Press

Published by Transatlantic Press
First published in 2012

Transatlantic Press
38 Copthorne Road
Croxley Green
Hertfordshire
WD3 4AQ

© Transatlantic Press
Photographs © Getty Images

ISBN 978-1-908533-39-5

Printed and bound in China

Contents

Introduction

The date: July 13, 1985. The time: 6.00pm. The place: Wembley Stadium, London. Queen take to the stage at Live Aid, and in a barnstorming 20-minute set confirm their status as stadium supergroup without equal. The 75,000-strong crowd aren't all Queen fans, yet Freddie Mercury, at his strutting, imperious, regal best, has them eating out of his palm. They sing, sway and clap at his ringmasterly bidding. The artists who shared the bill that day, major stars all, acknowledge that on this occasion they were tantamount to Queen support acts. Twenty years later, this Live Aid performance will be voted best live gig ever.

Queen had emerged during glam rock's heyday, a decade before that seminal Wembley appearance. Make-up and androgyny were almost de rigueur when "Seven Seas of Rhye" gave them their first hit in 1974. But Queen had serious musical depth underpinning the surface glitter. Brian May was a virtuoso guitarist, weaving fretboard magic on his homemade instrument. Blond pretty-boy Roger Taylor had percussion skills to match his teen-idol looks. John Deacon was a seasoned, polished bassist when he joined the band in 1971. And Freddie, a gifted pianist, had displayed his charismatic frontman credentials with several groups in his pre-Queen, pre-Mercury days.

If Freddie was the most outré of the four, someone with his sights set beyond mere stardom – his aim was "to be a legend" – the collective strength of the band can be seen in the songwriting credits. May penned "We Will Rock You" and "Hammer to Fall"; Taylor contributions include "Radio Ga Ga" and "A Kind of Magic"; Deacon supplied "Another One Bites the Dust" and "I Want to Break Free"; Mercury gave us "Killer Queen" and "We Are the Champions". Plus, of course, "Bohemian Rhapsody", which not only figures prominently in assorted "best ever" lists, but also upped the ante substantially in the field of video promos. Who else would put out a six-minute-long single mixing hard rock and operatic grandeur? Not even the Beatles can match such four-way, hit-writing prowess.

Queen racked up 39 UK Top 40 hits and seven chart-topping long-players prior to Freddie's death in 1991. Their *Greatest Hits* collection is the biggest-selling UK album of all time. The music crossed continents and the band followed. Queen shows were not just aural feasts, they were spectacles of bravura theatricality. As Freddie put it: "We're the Cecil B. DeMille of rock 'n' roll." Their output spans hard-driving rockers, gospel-inspired and disco-infused numbers, jaunty period pieces, rockabilly, anthemic blockbusters and tender ballads. Yet for all its diversity, the canon bears an unmistakable stamp, be it the inimitable sound of Brian's "Red Special", Freddie's distinctive vocals or soaring harmonies mimicking a full-blown choir. Taking risks and moving forward was central to the band's creative code. Repeating even a winning formula was anathema to their musical credo.

Such extraordinary success and longevity alone would have assured Queen a place at rock music's top table. But having Freddie Mercury out in front set them apart even from such rarefied company. No one played to the crowd – played with the crowd – like Freddie. The image underwent several changes; the electrifying showmanship was evident from first to last. His private life was turbulent, replete with rock-star excess. He struggled to come to terms with his sexuality, and by the time he found monogamous contentment, the AIDS time bomb was already ticking.

Freddie Mercury always felt it was more important to live a fabulous life than a long one. He made good on that self-pledge, and in the process helped Queen carve a unique place in the annals of rock 'n' roll.

Chapter One

Keep Yourself Alive

Making overtures

As the 60s drew to a close, Freddie Bulsara was a fan of Smile, a band that included Brian May and Roger Taylor. He was ever willing to dispense advice, not least how the band would gain from having him as its frontman. Freddie sang with other bands – Ibex, Wreckage and Sour Milk Sea – biding his time until the slot he really wanted became available. The departure of Smile's vocalist Tim Staffell early in 1970 paved the way for Freddie to add the pizzazz he felt they were lacking.

Once Freddie achieved what he had long been angling for and joined May and Taylor's band, it heralded a change of name. Freddie Bulsara became Freddie Mercury. Some made the mythological connection: Mercury, the winged messenger of the Roman gods. Others said it was rooted in astrology, Mercury being his ruling planet. Or maybe it was from a line in one of Freddie's songs. Whatever the case, "changing his name helped him assume a different skin," said Brian of the band mate who was adept at reinventing himself. It was Freddie, too, who suggested the name Queen. "It was a very regal name and it sounded splendid. It's strong, very universal and immediate. It had a lot of visual potential and was open to all sorts of interpretations."

Head in the clouds

In his youth Brian May was pulled in twin directions: stars and stardom. The studious grammar schoolboy from Feltham, Middlesex, was mad keen on astronomy, and an academic career beckoned. In 1965 he began a degree course at London's Imperial College of Science and Technology, the next step on the road to becoming a fully-fledged astrophysicist. But by then he had also been bitten by the rock and roll bug. Already an accomplished guitarist, May had gravitated from jamming with school friends to playing in a band called 1984, whose number included fellow Hampton Grammar School pupil Tim Staffell. 1984 had some notable engagements, twice sharing a bill with Jimi Hendrix in 1967. May and Staffell left in quick succession, hooking up to form a new band, Smile. It was another stepping-stone on the path that led to the formation of Queen.

Skins and teeth

Queen's pin-up boy and one of the twin drivers of the rhythm section. Roger Taylor spent his early years in East Anglia before the family relocated to Truro, Cornwall, where he was a chorister at the city's Cathedral School. After dabbling with the guitar, he took up the drumsticks and went on to make his name on the local circuit, notably with The Reaction, eventually taking over as the band's lead vocalist. Autumn 1967 saw 18-year-old Taylor move to the capital to begin a dentistry course at London Hospital Medical School. A year later, The Reaction having disintegrated, he answered an advertisement for a "Ginger Baker/Mitch Mitchell-type drummer", posted by one Brian May. Taylor was now a member of Smile, though it would be two more years before the band was rebadged as Queen, three before its line-up was complete.

Designs on a performing career

Freddie, pictured in 1969, the year he left Ealing College of Art with a diploma in graphic art and design. He had little enthusiasm for using his qualifications in a professional capacity ("When I was finished with the illustrating course, I was sick of it. I'd had it up to here"). His mind was soon set on a performing career, emulating the achievements of his idol, Jimi Hendrix, whom he sketched endlessly during his college days. At school he had learned piano, reaching Grade 4 standard, but his ability on guitar hardly matched Hendrix's virtuosity. He mastered only a few rudimentary chords, though a decade later these would be enough for him to compose "Crazy Little Thing Called Love", which gave Queen their first No. 1 in America in 1979. It became a staple in their live set, the only time Freddie picked up a guitar on stage.

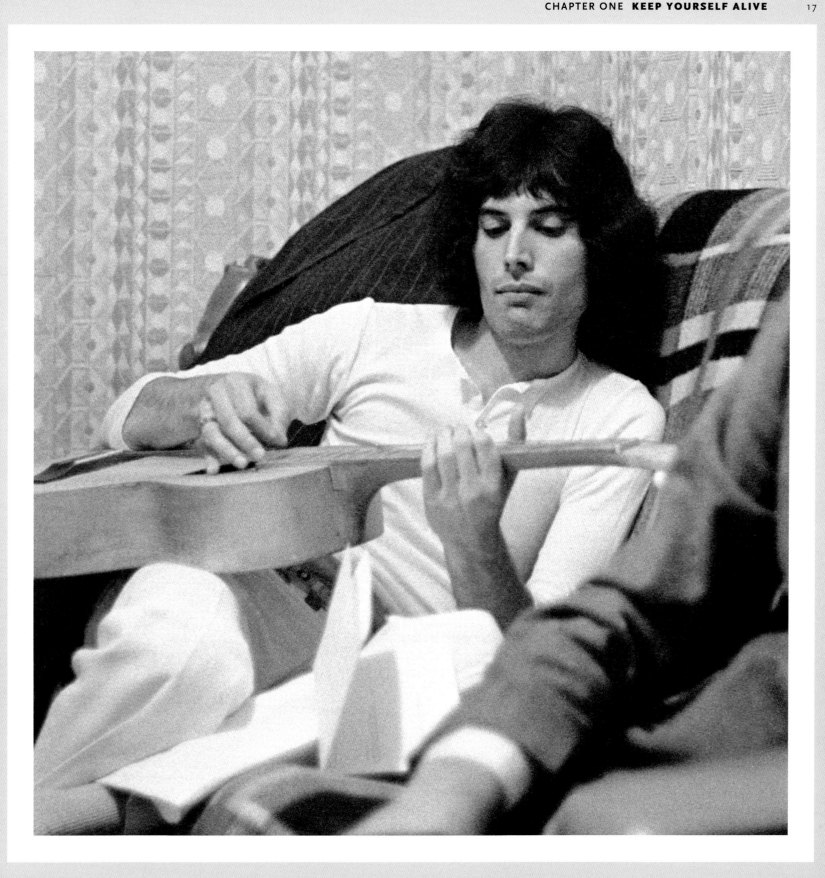

"I Can Hear Music"

What was Queen's debut on vinyl? In 1969, during their Smile incarnation, the band signed a deal with Mercury Records, which yielded the single "Earth"/"Step On Me". It was released in August that year, but only in America. Unsurprisingly, an unplugged record made by a group of overseas unknowns raised barely a ripple. Even if it had, it would scarcely have counted, since neither Freddie Mercury nor John Deacon were yet part of the line-up. Four years on, "Keep Yourself Alive" and their eponymous debut album, both released in July 1973, marked the band's first outing on EMI. But the intervening time threw up a recording curiosity. During their early days with Trident, while kicking their heels waiting for a studio slot, Mercury, May and Taylor were recruited by one of the studio's producers to perform on a cover of the Beach Boys hit "I Can Hear Music". It was released in June 1973 – just before Queen's own debut single and album – under the name Larry Lurex, a cash-in on the then current trend for all things glitter. That, too, did little business, and Freddie & Co. had only a session fee to show for it.

The Red Special

Opposite: For many fans Brian's guitar sound is as much a Queen signature as Freddie's vocals. Having added a pick-up to the acoustic guitar he received for his seventh birthday, Brian and his father, Harold, set to work on a more ambitious project when the besotted youngster wanted to go electric. It took almost two years to hand-craft the Red Special, as it came to be known, using miscellaneous scrap materials that came to hand. These included an old fireplace and table for the neck and body, part of a bicycle saddlebag, motorcycle springs and a knitting needle! Speaking in the early 90s, when the world-famous instrument was almost 30 years old, May was as enamoured as ever with his art: "I love the sound of the guitar. I love standing there making that noise. It's just as much a release for me now as it was when I was a kid."

Right: Zandra Rhodes designed many of the flamboyant stage outfits worn by Queen during the mid-70s. They included this pleated-top-and-satin-flares number, created for the 1974 Earls Court concert, which gave an impressive wingspan befitting pop music's most outré performer.

"I like to ham it up"

On stage c. 1975. Although Queen rose to prominence during the glam rock era, their musicianship, complex song structures and sophisticated lyrics placed them far ahead of other bands who reached for the make-up and nail varnish. Androgyny was in, and Freddie camped it up on stage for all he was worth. The theatricality left a lot of critics cold, but Freddie in particular recognized the importance of creating a spectacle. "I like to ham it up. I like to really perform a song. It's my job to make sure that I win them over and make them feel that they've had a good time." It was a position of power and influence, and Freddie knew better than anyone how to play an audience. "How they loved to twitch at the tip of his invisible lash," one reviewer observed. But away from the spotlight he could be reserved and shy, and spoke of his stage persona – often overtly sexual and arrogant – as a monster he'd created.

Bass mettle

John Deacon was Queen's youngest member and the last to join the band. Born in a suburb of Leicester, Deacon was an unassuming, academic youngster, keen on electronics, which he went on to study at Chelsea College. He joined a school band called The Opposition, which played the local club circuit, and was a seasoned gigger by the time he moved to London to begin his degree course in 1969. Deacon had started out on guitar, taking up bass to plug a gap in The Opposition line-up, and was a polished player by the time he came within Queen's orbit. He actually saw his future band mates play as a paying punter in October 1970, and wasn't overly impressed. Queen had gone through several bass players, one of whom is said to have been shown the door for indulging in stage antics that undermined Freddie's posturing. An accomplished but unshowy player was needed to augment the rhythm section. By February 1971, a mutual friend put Deacon in touch with the band. Queen finally had their man – and an electronics wiz to boot!

Stand and deliver

Left: Freddie cavorts with the top half of the microphone stand, a prop he made ample use of. He toyed with one during Queen's *Top of the Pops* performance of "Killer Queen" in autumn 1974, stroking the chrome shaft suggestively in his delivery of the song that put the band firmly on the map, rising to No. 2 in the UK. For once, it wasn't a premeditated piece of Mercury showmanship. A mic stand had come to pieces in his hand during a gig, and only after Freddie was left holding the upper section did he see, and milk, the possibilities.

Opposite: With his home-made Red Special, which he played with a sixpence coin instead of a plectrum, Brian established himself among the pantheon of guitar gods. But 1974, the year that ended with "Killer Queen's" parent album *Sheer Heart Attack* also hitting the No. 2 spot, had been a trying one for May. He contracted an arm infection that turned gangrenous during a trip to Australia at the beginning of the year, and was struck down with hepatitis during a spring tour of the US supporting Mott the Hoople. On top of that, Queen were making precious little money from the deal they had signed with Trident Audio Productions in 1972. May, who had abandoned his PhD on the zodiacal dust cloud and also flirted briefly with a teaching career, risked disappointing parents who were concerned he was throwing away a valuable educational investment, wasting enormous potential. Only later, said May, when he flew them aboard Concorde to watch a Queen show in New York, did they finally see why their son had chosen music over academe.

Conflicted over sexuality

Freddie strikes a suggestive pose, mirroring Brian's stance during a guitar break. If the flamboyant frontman's antics raised questions about his sexuality to the casual observer – was it mere glam-era stagecraft or something deeper? – then those close to him were equally uncertain regarding his predilections. "At the time I didn't know Freddie was gay," said Brian in a 2011 interview, "and I don't know if he did either." The man who littered his utterances with "darling" when addressing both sexes had several girlfriends, notably Mary Austin, whom he met when she was working at London's celebrated Biba fashion store. They were a serious item for some years and remained close throughout his life, Mercury referring to her as his "common law wife". That he suppressed his homosexuality for some considerable time was almost certainly down to his Zoroastrian upbringing. According to the tenets of that faith, gay relationships are sinful, and Freddie's abiding love for his parents, Bomi and Jer, ensured that he maintained a compartmentalized lifestyle .

Naturally diffident

Above: With rock star status comes adulation and plenty of female attention. Exuberant on stage, Brian May was no extrovert away from the spotlight. One of the attractions of the guitar for May the gangly schoolboy was as a prop to counter his natural diffidence.

Opposite: Queen pictured in May 1975.

Creative disharmony

Brian May swaps the Red Special for a Fender Stratocaster for this performance on Dutch television in 1975. May's rocker "Now I'm Here", culled from *Sheer Heart Attack* as the follow-up to "Killer Queen", reached No. 11 in the UK chart at the beginning of the year. After a spring tour that also took in Japan, where Queenmania was rampant, the band set to work on their next album. The four would work separately and bring ideas to the table for consideration by the group in an atmosphere of competitive creativity. They would argue about minuscule details as they strove for perfection; a single note could spark a row. "If we didn't disagree," said Freddie, "we'd just be yes-men – and we do get the cream in the end." The one thing they set their face against was reworking old formulae, an accusation no one could level as their next long-player, *A Night at the Opera*, took shape.

Single issue

Queen, pictured in 1975, the year *A Night at the Opera* "took off like a rocket", as Brian May put it. The album was a game-changer both artistically and financially. Queen didn't consciously write singles; they'd focus on producing an album, from which a consensus view of which track would make a single would emerge. There were inevitably disagreements, however, and naturally the writer of a particular song would make the case for his baby. Brian May said that on Opera he had a particular fondness for "'39", a wild rover-type folk song in a galactic setting, but "Bohemian Rhapsody" and "You're My Best Friend" were chosen from the 11-song set. Somewhat ruefully, Brian noted that once such decisions were made and those not selected consigned to remain as album tracks, their chance of wider exposure and the opportunity to stake a place in people's consciousness disappeared for good.

As well as "Bohemian Rhapsody" and the vitriolic "Death on Two Legs", Freddie's contribution to *A Night at the Opera* also included the jaunty, period-feel pair "Lazing on a Sunday Afternoon" and "Seaside Rendezvous, plus the beautiful ballad "Love of My Life", written for Mary Austin and featuring Brian on harp.

Royal seal

Above: Roger Taylor in full flow in 1975. With three science-orientated band members, unsurprisingly, it fell to the artistically-minded Freddie to come up with the logo that adorned Roger's bass drum, the album covers and all manner of merchandise. His design incorporated the band members' birth signs: a pair of lions for Leos Roger and John, a crab for Cancerian Brian and two fairies for the Virgoan frontman himself. Add in the letter Q encircling a crown, and open-winged phoenix overseeing proceedings and it makes for a quality-assured crest full of pomp and the stamp of majesty.

Opposite: Brian at the Hammersmith Odeon, London, 29 November 1975. That year he was approached by Sparks, a band consisting of brothers Russell and Ron Mael, who had scored hits with songs such as "This Town Ain't Big Enough for the Both of Us", which reached No. 2 the previous year. Queen had actually supported Sparks at London's Marquee Club in 1972, when both bands were trying to make their name. While Sparks reached their peak with that first hit, certainly in terms of chart success, innumerable glittering triumphs lay ahead for Queen.

On being vocal

John Deacon has stated that had his sole input been as bass player, it would have limited the level of satisfaction he derived from being part of the group. Writing songs and being part of the decision making process made it much more rewarding. His first writing credit came with "Misfire" on *Sheer Heart Attack*, and within two years he would have a Top 10 hit to his name. Though he is pictured (above) addressing a microphone, John's vocal ability fell well short of the other three Queen members. "It's the one thing I wish I could do – sing – because it would make songwriting so much easier." As for being part of the decision making, that grew over time. In the early days he felt something of an outsider, the "new boy" who didn't want to push himself forward. He often stood quietly on the fringes as the other three made their views known, in what was often a heated forum. His laid-back attitude extended to allowing himself to be credited "Deacon John" on Queen's eponymous debut album, which the others thought a more interesting take on his name.

Top of the Pops

Opposite and above: Queen perform on *Top of the Pops*. In the early days, when they were desperate to raise their profile, the band looked on an appearance on the BBC's flagship music programme as a major, career-boosting coup. Once they were established, turning up at a studio to mime to a record or a backing track had little appeal. Thus, after showcasing "Seven Seas of Rhye", "Killer Queen" and "Now I'm Here" on *Top of the Pops*, the band chose a different promotional vehicle with their fourth single. The video for "Bohemian Rhapsody", shot in four hours at a cost of £4,000, received its first airing on the show on November 20, 1975, three weeks after the single's release. Filmed at Elstree Studios and directed by Bruce Gowers – who had shot their Live at the Rainbow concert the previous year – the video contained effects and imagery that were groundbreaking at the time. The dazzling visuals created a buzz that sent sales of "Bo Rhap" – already healthy – rocketing. Music videos would never be the same again.

Chapter Two

We Are The Champions

A Day at the Races

Above and opposite: The huge international success of *A Night at the Opera* and "Bohemian Rhapsody" was followed by the release of the album *A Day at the Races* in December 1976. Where else would Queen go to promote the album but Kempton Park, one of England's premier racetracks? To Freddie and Mary Austin's left is the band's manager John Reid, whom Freddie said inspired the track "The Millionaire Waltz".

Brian attends with Chrissy Mullen, the long-term girlfriend whom he married in May that year. The lead single from their first self-produced album, "Somebody to Love", was a typically lush production. By contrast, Freddie's "You Take My Breath Away" showed that they could also deliver a simple, spare song. They weren't wedded to multiple overdubs and complex arrangements, said Freddie. "If it needs it, we do it."

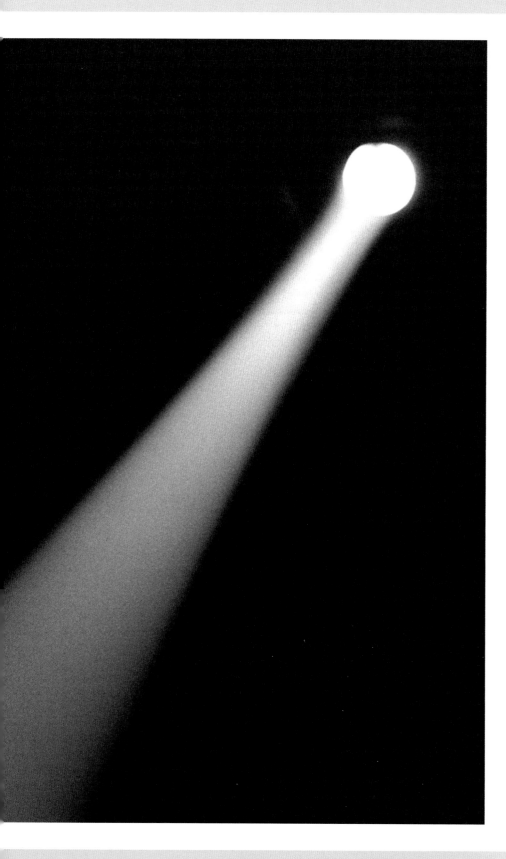

Attention to detail

Brian's first exposure to the guitar family was the ukulele-banjo, an instrument made famous by George Formby, which his father played. When he received his first acoustic guitar for his seventh birthday, Brian quickly got to work transposing the chords he'd been shown onto his six-string instrument. He used that early grounding to good effect in the song "Good Company" from *A Night at the Opera*, in which he not only played the uke but used guitar effects to create a complete brass section. By his own admission it was painstaking work, but he is temperamentally suited to such assiduous attention to detail. Brian once said perfectionism was both his best and worst trait.

"I need somebody to love"

Left and opposite: Queen performing at New York's Madison Square Garden, an iconic venue that became a regular stop-off on tours of America after the band made its debut there in February 1977. The recently released *A Day at the Races* was conceived as a companion piece to *A Night at the Opera*, the link reinforced by the titular Marx Brothers connection. It gave Queen their second UK chart-topping album. Lead single, the gospel-inspired "Somebody to Love", was Freddie paying homage to Aretha Franklin. It didn't quite match "Bohemian Rhapsody", either in terms of chart position – peaking at No. 2 in the UK – or in terms of vocal overdubs (the latter had around 180, with the tape turning almost transparent); but the choral effect was no less impressive, and Freddie regarded "Somebody to Love" as a better song than "Bo Rhap". The song's title and soaring refrain had a yearning, soul-searching quality that addressed both divine and earthly matters. It was around the time of its release that Freddie put his relationship with Mary Austin on a platonic footing, freeing him to explore new relationships.

Words and music

By the end of the 70s, the majority of Queen's singles had
been down to Freddie. He liked to write quickly to maintain a
freshness and spontaneity; to capture the essence of a song
quickly before the sedulous business of adding the polish.
"Crazy Little Thing Called Love" was one composition that was
completed in a matter of minutes. "Bohemian Rhapsody", he
said, was an amalgamation of three separate songs, blended
into a matchless entity. If an idea wasn't working, Freddie
would happily abandon or shelve it. He found melodies easier
to come by than lyrics, the latter often containing a fantasy
element. Some have speculated as to whether the cocaine
habit he developed played a part in the creative process.
The "airy-fairy" lyrics certainly came under the microscope,
but Freddie waved away all questions about interpretation.
That was for the listener to decide. "If you see it, dears, then
it's there," said the man who called "Bohemian Rhapsody"
"random rhyming nonsense". Nor did he have any inflated
sense of the value of his art. Self-effacingly, he compared his
songs to disposable razors, to be consumed and replaced in
short order.

The "Queen Lizzy" tour

Above: January 1977 saw Queen embark on an exhaustive two-month tour of America and Canada on the back of the recently released *Day at the Races* album. Supporting them was Thin Lizzy, whose frontman Phil Lynott is pictured with Roger Taylor and John Deacon. It was a risk choosing a band as good as Lizzy to open for them – one newspaper dubbed it "the rock package to beat them all". They had been due to headline their own American tour until one of the band became indisposed, and the fact that guitar great and former Lizzy band member Gary Moore was drafted in as replacement showed that they were no easy outfit to upstage. Speaking of the decision, Roger Taylor said Lizzy were a better fit with Queen audiences than some of the other possible choices. Why choose a folk singer and make life easy for yourself, he opined, when there was the chance to have a top-drawer double bill. "If I was a rock 'n' roll fan, I would go and see this show if it came to my town. Definitely."

Put your hands together

Above and opposite: Freddy pictured in Copenhagen in 1977. Freddie's "We are the Champions", which hit the UK No. 2 spot in autumn 1977, has become one of the great sporting anthems, reverberating around stadiums as fans join together in celebratory outpouring. It was Brian May who first had the idea to write a song specifically geared to mass participation. He noticed that fans were chanting the lyrics to the songs, something unusual for rock concerts of the time, and came up with "We Will Rock You" to acknowledge 'that our audience had become part of the show, and we could no longer just regard it as a one-way experience'. The rhythmic clapping and stomping were, in true Queen style, overdubbed repeatedly to give a pulsating, saturated sound. "We Will Rock You" went out as the B-side to "We are the Champions", both songs featuring on the 1977 News of the World album. It was released as a double A-side in America, where it reached No. 4 on the Billboard chart. These twin anthems, which became staples of Queen's live set, usually played in tandem, were admitted to the Grammy Hall of Fame in 2009.

A kind of magic

February 1977, Omni Coliseum, Atlanta, Georgia.
Roger Taylor said that his, Brian's and Freddie's voices "interacted quite magically".
Rather than simply take a vocal part each, they would often all sing each part to
cover all harmonising bases. Overdubs and multi-tracking were used extensively to
create a lush, layered sound that could pass for a large choir. The band paid special
tribute to the studio wizardry of Mike Stone and Roy Thomas Baker, who helped
them capture their sonic ideas on vinyl in the 70s, before they took to recording
overseas. If *A Night at the Opera* was Queen's *Sgt Pepper*, to use Brian's analogy,
then Stone and Baker can be seen as the band's George Martin. Baker worked on
the first four Queen albums, returning to co-produce their 1978 long-player, *Jazz*.
Stone was at the mixing desk for the first six albums, up to and including *News
of the World*, when he was finally accorded co-producer status. In his eulogy on
learning of Stone's death in 2002, Brian singled out "Millionaire Waltz" from *A
Day at the Races* as an exemplar of their early studio collaborator's special gifts.
Where most people might have singled out the better known "Somebody to Love",
which featured on the same album, May thought this track "an even more amazing
painting in sound on a broad canvas".

Paying dividends

February 1977: On stage in Atlanta during Queen's North
American Day at the Races tour. In addition to the hits, the set
list included "Brighton Rock", "The Prophet's Song", "Ogre
Battle" and "Stone Cold Crazy". Plus, of course, the "God Save
the Queen" finale, the outro on *A Night at the Opera* which had
become a show-closing fixture since the 1975 tour of America.
They also performed "Death on Two Legs", whose barbed lyrics
were inspired by the band's disastrous contractual dealings
with Trident. Songs that made it onto the Queen catalogue were
credited to the band member who brought it to the table, and
that person profited accordingly. Thus, Roger Taylor racked up
enormous earnings by having the good fortune of having his
composition "I'm In Love with My Car" selected as the B-side
to "Bohemian Rhapsody". This arrangement prevailed until
1989 and the release of *The Miracle* album, the first to be jointly
credited to all four individuals.

Rhapsody in blue

Opposite: Performing in Copenhagen, May 1977. In Queen Elizabeth II's Silver Jubilee year, Queen scooped the British Phonographic Industry award for Best Single of the Last 25 Years for "Bohemian Rhapsody", an honour shared with Procul Harum's "A Whiter Shade of Pale" (the two songs are also lyrically linked, by the word "fandango"). A Queen's Award to Industry given to EMI in 1978 prompted the company to press a commemorative 200 copies of "Bo Rhap", reflecting the fact that Queen's overseas sales had played no small part in an award given for export earnings. It was the obvious choice, though EMI executives hadn't been quite so enthusiastic when the six-minute song was mooted as a single three years before. These commemorative records, issued on blue vinyl, are among the most prized items sought by collectors of Queen memorabilia.

Left: "I dress to kill, but tastefully, and I have fun with my clothes on stage. It's not just a concert you're seeing, it's a fashion show too."

Excess capacity

Above: "Each new number needs to be expressed visually as well as musically, and we couldn't bear the show to be the same every time." Freddie was invariably the focal point of that visual expression, but there were some impressive props to enhance the spectacle. Their 1977 European tour, which ended with two concerts at London's Earls Court, saw the introduction of a £50,000, crown-shaped lighting rig that would rise majestically from the stage amid plumes of smoke. The post-gig festivities were no less lavish. Queen parties became the stuff of legend,

tales circulating of dwarfs carrying bowls of cocaine for guests to dip into, female mud wrestling and a nude model served up on a platter, covered by cuts of meat. There was plenty of money rolling in to pay for such entertainment. The band's earnings were such that they would pay crippling rates of tax if they remained in Britain more than 10 weeks per year, an issue they addressed by recording in a number of overseas studios.

Opposite: Freddy stikes a dramatic pose, Copenghagen, May 1977.

Call me Mister Fahrenheit

Above: Freddie, pictured with Mary Austin in October 1977, the central female figure in his adult life. "I couldn't fall in love with a man the same way as I have with Mary," he said. "I'll love her until I draw my last breath." Having ended their relationship – on a romantic level, at least – he engaged in countless casual dalliances, a pattern of reckless indulgence that lasted for several years. His unfettered hedonism was reflected in the lyric of "Don't Stop Me Now", a UK Top 10 hit in 1979. Brian May called the song "a stroke of genius", though the licentious lifestyle it espoused,

and which Freddie voraciously adopted, had already set alarm bells ringing.

Opposite: Though he was one of rock music's most flamboyant characters, Freddie largely eschewed the glitzy, celeb party circuit. When performing in New York or recording in Munich, cities with a flourishing gay scene, he hit the nightspots with a vengeance. Over time there would be long-term male lovers, but also a succession of one-off encounters.

Not quite so rock 'n'roll

Opposite and above: Little surprise that the members of Queen show an interest in photography, given that they set such store by the visual aspect of the music business. Away from the legendary wild parties and spending sprees, there were other pastimes and preoccupations that were not quite so rock 'n' roll. The four enjoyed a competitive game of Scrabble, and over the years Freddie would lavish much attention on his ornate Japanese garden, koi carp and pet cats.

Chain reaction

Freddie's song "Bicycle Race" is one of the few where the genesis is well documented. It was written in 1978, when for tax reasons Queen relocated to France to make their seventh album, *Jazz*, the first to be recorded beyond England's shores. They worked at Mountain Studios in Montreux – which they would later purchase – and also a facility in Nice. It was while at the latter studio that Freddie witnessed the hoop-la as the Tour de France passed through the resort. It inspired him to write "Bicycle Race", which was paired with Brian's "Fat Bottomed Girls" for the album's lead single. The promo film, featuring a bevy of naked models riding around Wimbledon Stadium, stirred up something of a hornet's nest. Technical effects were used to maintain decorum in the video, but a poster insert in the album showing the riders in all their glory caused considerable controversy, especially in the United States. The "offensive" material was removed, purchasers having to apply in writing if they wished to receive a copy. The single sleeve, which originally featured a naked derriere, also had to be doctored to assuage the outraged.

new album
EMC 3061
OC 062 96528

also available on ca

May flowers

Opposite: Along with Freddie, Brian May took the lion's share of the songwriting credits in the early years. His hard-rocking numbers "Now I'm Here and "Tie Your Mother Down" both made the singles chart, as did "We Will Rock You" and "Fat Bottomed Girls", while Queen albums contained liberal helpings of May compositions, including "Keep Yourself Alive" – the song that helped launch their career – and "Brighton Rock". He wrote "Tie Your Mother Down" while pursuing his academic studies on Tenerife, when he was still trying to weigh the twin callings of astronomy and pop music. He certainly looked the part of pop star. While Freddie went through several image makeovers, Brian maintained his trademark bouffant mop. Growing up, he didn't like the wild, frizzy look, but came round to curls after Hendrix made them cool. As well as being linked by their coiffure and standing among the all-time great guitarists, the two also have national anthems in common: Brian's signature performance of "God Save the Queen" mirrored Hendrix's famous rendition of the "Star-Spangled Banner" at Woodstock in '69.

Right: Roger Taylor was the main man during Queen's early shows in Cornwall. An established name in his home county, he took top billing as the local "legendary" drummer, Queen relegated to the role of backing band.

Taylor made

Roger Taylor leaves his drumkit to take centre stage with Freddie. A multi-instrumentalist, Taylor had numerous writing credits to his name during the 70s, including "Tenement Funster", "Drowse" and "Sheer Heart Attack". His monster A-side successes still lay ahead, but his "I'm in Love with My Car", the flipside of "Bohemian Rhapsody", was a concert favourite. His distinctive, high-register voice figured prominently on "Bo-Rhap", notably with his rendition of "for me" at the end of the operatic section. Taylor demonstrated his impressive multi-octave range on many Queen tracks, invariably taking lead vocals on his own songs. He was the first member of the band to launch a solo career, releasing the single "I Wanna Testify" in 1977. His 1981 album *Fun in Space*, also a first, made the UK Top 20, and he later toured and recorded with his own band, The Cross, when Queen were taking a break.

Read all about it

Left and opposite: Queen's American label, Elektra, throws a party to celebrate the band's sixth studio album, *News of the World*, which made the Top 5 on both sides of the Atlantic and topped several other national charts. Musically eclectic, their 1977 album also showed off the band's individual talents: it has John playing six-string, Roger strapping on a bass, while Brian takes lead vocal and plays piano on "All Dead, All Dead". Brian and Roger are seen thumbing a copy of the October 1953 issue of *Astounding Science Fiction*, which inspired the sleeve artwork. The man behind the magazine cover was the doyen of sci-fi illustrators, Frank Kelly Freas (1922–2005), who was commissioned to revisit his earlier work and amend it for the album cover.

On the road

Roger Taylor, surrounded by just some of the gear
Queen took on the road during their 1977 American
tour. Not all of it survived the trip. At the finale
of the Madison Square Garden gig he ploughed
straight through his drumkit, trashing a £400
microphone in the process. Taylor spoke of the
band's apprehension at including their latest hit,
"Somebody to Love", in the show. "There are so
many voices on the record that I didn't know if we'd
be able to do it. I enjoy playing it now, but when we
first started the tour we were dreading it when it
came round in the set. I suppose we've got over the
barrier of reproducing tracks live. I mean, we'll have
a go at anything." Queen didn't confine themselves
to their own music when they went on the road.
"Jailhouse Rock" and "Big Spender" were set-list
regulars on this tour and many others.

Playing to the crowd

Opposite and right: Freddie was somewhat dismissive of his ability on the piano, and over time played less and less on stage as he focused on ramping it up out in front. "Love of My Life", for example, was written on piano but adapted for guitar on stage to allow Freddie to concentrate on vocals. It was an arrangement the band felt worked best when in performance mode, but perhaps didn't show off Freddie's full range of talents to the best of their ability. Brian said he had a delightful touch on the keyboards, while Roger commented that being labelled a charismatic showman often masked the fact that Freddie was a brilliant musician.

Taking care of business

Above: Live at Copenhagen's Broendby Hall, May 12, 1977 and (opposite) at Earls Court, London, in June. By now Queen were reaping the dividends of their enormous success, the post-"Killer Queen" penury replaced by separate limos to speed them to and from gigs. When those wouldn't suffice, a helicopter would take up the slack. The transformation in their fortunes was in no small part down to John Reid, Elton John's manager, who took care of the business side after the Trident deal was terminated.

It was he who freed them from the cares of the balance sheet, allowing them the time and space to make A *Night at the Opera*. By the time Reid severed his links with the band early in 1978 – an amicable parting of the ways born of the fact that Queen were now such a huge brand that he couldn't devote sufficient time to their dealings – they were well on their way to a place in the *Guinness Book of Records* for their eye-watering executive earnings from Queen Productions Ltd.

We grafted

Roger Taylor had the wherewithal to be a pin-up frontman in his own right, carrying on from his early days in the spotlight on the Cornwall music circuit. There was a serious work ethic underpinning the dreamy looks, established when Queen were a hungry young band and continuing even when success came their way. In a 2011 interview for *Q* magazine, he spoke of the band's assiduous approach to record making in those heady early days. "It was almost like a privilege to get in these studios which, at the time, cost what seemed like a fortune. Thirty quid for every hour! So we respected that and just grafted." Such effort delivered seven albums in six years, a level of industriousness that paid handsome dividends. The wintry performance video for the 1978 single "Spread Your Wings" was shot in the garden of Taylor's Surrey home.

Going solo

Opposite: January 26, 1977: Limbering up backstage at the Montreal Forum, the first Canadian date of the Day at the Races North American tour. With just a handful of his songs making it on to Queen's first five albums, Roger Taylor that year became the first band member to issue a solo record. He had a batch of songs to choose from when this three-month tour ended and thoughts turned to studio work. They included "Sheer Heart Attack" – still in embryonic form when the album of the same name was completed – and "Fight from the Inside". In the event, both songs made the cut for Queen's next long-player, *News of the World*. That left "I Wanna Testify" and "Turn on the TV", which became the A and B-sides of Taylor's debut single, released August 1977. "I Wanna Testify", a funk rehash of a song originally recorded by The Parliaments a decade earlier, failed to chart.

Left: Brian suffered a number of health scares as Queen broke through into the big time, and a massage is just the ticket to help prepare for the onerous 1977 touring schedule. Queen played 85 shows that year, a European tour separating two trips to America.

Significant others

"I'm just a true romantic," said Freddie, declaring that emotion was the unifying theme of all his songs. If he wasn't the first person to make that claim, he used emotional experiences to produce words and music bearing his own special hallmark. Those experiences included a relationship with Joe Fanelli, a one-time chef who remained part of Freddie's household retinue after their romance had ended. Another key figure in Freddie's life was Peter Freestone, a wardrobe assistant he met when he worked with the Royal Ballet in 1979. Initially employed as wardrobe man when Queen went on the road, Freestone eventually became Freddie's general factotum. Dubbed "Phoebe" by Mercury – after his fashion of giving many of his close male friends a female moniker – Freestone, like "Liza" Fanelli, would remain a trusted member of the singer's inner circle for the remainder of his life.

Parallels with "Sharon"

Opposite: Freddie, pictured with showbiz pals Elton John and Peter Straker. Elton John – or "Sharon", as Freddie called him – was an enduring friend, the two having much in common apart from rock star status, flamboyant stage persona and piano prowess. Like Freddie, Elton had reinvented himself, casting off his Reginald Dwight identity during his rise to the top. While Freddie fretted over his pronounced overbite, Elton also had body-image issues. And both men were conflicted over their orientation, John going a step further than Freddie had with Mary Austin by marrying Renate Blauel in 1984. Peter Straker became part of Freddie's circle in the mid-70s. A Jamaica-born actor with musical ambitions, Straker cut an album called *This One's On Me* in 1978, funded and produced by his superstar friend. The peak of his pop career came in 1987, when he performed backing vocals on Freddie's Top 10 solo hit "The Great Pretender", and also appeared in the video – inevitably in drag.

Above: Freddie with Todd Rundgren. Freddie said in the early days he wore black nail varnish, make-up and outfits that made a grand entrance a certainty.

All that Jazz

Left: Hamburg, April 14, 1978. A study in concentration from a consummate guitarist during Queen's second News of the World tour, a month-long, whistle-stop lap of Europe following on from the previous year's North American shows. When the tour was over, the band started work on their next album, *Jazz*, which confounded many critics, not least for its eclectic mix that had barely a nod towards the titular genre. The first two singles did well, the double A-side "Bicycle Race"/"Fat Bottomed Girls" peaking at No. 11 in the UK, and follow-up "Don't Stop Me Now" hitting No. 9. But "Jealousy" and "Mustapha", released in selective markets, hit the buffers, and none of the 45s made the Top 20 in America, where Queen's stock had fallen in the wake of the "Bicycle Race" poster furore. With songs such as "Mustapha", the album's Arabic-flavoured opener, Queen showed themselves once again to be prepared to go out on a limb rather than play safe. *Rolling Stone* called it "clumsy and pretentious". Queen were used to riling the critics, Freddie opining that favourable coverage was important only at the beginning of a band's career. "When success arrives, it's the fans who decide." Sure enough, *Jazz* played well with those whose opinion he valued most, rising to No. 2 in the UK album chart, No. 6 in America.

Opposite: Roger Taylor pictured at the Oakland Coliseum, California, in December 1978.

Holding court

Opposite and above: Rocking out in Inglewood, California, December 1978, when Queen hit the road on the back of the *Jazz* album, their seventh studio long-player. Its predecessor, *News of the World*, broke a lengthy sequence in faring better in America than the band's home market, though only marginally; it made the top five on both sides of the Atlantic. In barely four years Queen had scored nine UK Top 20 singles, while six albums had made the top five. They had a devoted worldwide following, yet the critics remained cool. The arrival of punk seemed only to render the music press more impervious to Queen's appeal. In one spiky interview for *New Musical Express*, Freddie defended his corner, insisting that Queen were intent on widening the boundaries of pop, and that the glitzy, stylised stage shows were inextricably bound to their sophisticated brand of music. Their fans, he said, wanted a theatrical experience, the full showbiz works, which Queen delivered in spades. 'Can you imagine doing the sort of songs that we've written, like "Rhapsody" or "Somebody to Love", in jeans, with absolutely no presentation?'

Biker chic

Opposite and right: Freddie sports a new look during the Jazz tour of America and Canada, autumn 1978. The hair is shorter. Out go the spangly leotards and balletic look, replaced by black PVC. Leather was also in, Freddie remarking: "I rather fancy myself as a black panther." He adopted the biker style that was popular in the gay nightspots he frequented in Munich and New York. "And of course, I wear it with panache."

On the drums

Above: Roger Taylor in full flow during the 1980 Jazz tour. Queen's eclecticism was a boon to Taylor, who felt the different styles of music they played was essential to maintaining stimulation and interest levels. Not for him the pounding repetitiveness that is the customary lot of a heavy metal drummer. By contrast, Brian May said that had the cards fallen differently he could easily have seen himself playing guitar with a band such as Australian hard-rocking outfit AC-DC. He had all the skills required of a top axeman, but not the physical make-up, he thought. "Wrong sort of size and shape."

Reflective moments

Freddie's complex, rollercoaster private life ran from free-living, free-loving self-indulgence to reflective moments when he was drawn to the attractions of simple family life. At times he pondered what it would be like to settle down and have a child. Mercury's own upbringing had fallen short of the ideal, and he ultimately realized he was temperamentally unsuited to the role of family man. "I'm much too restless and highly strung." If the urge to have a child became too strong, Freddie said he would "go to Harrods and buy one".

Mack and Munich

Left and opposite: Performing at Hamburg's Ernst Merck Halle, April 14, 1978. Germany would play an important part in Queen's recording career. They heard glowing reports of Munich's Musicland Studios, which had been founded by Giorgio Moroder and attracted bands of the calibre of Led Zeppelin. Taking the opportunity to record there brought them into contact with sound engineer-producer Reinhold Mack, whose credits included several ELO projects. The collaboration struck gold immediately as Freddie's "Crazy Little Think Called Love", dashed off in a matter of minutes while he was relaxing in the bath at his hotel suite, was recorded at Musicland with Mack at the mixing desk. This Elvis pastiche gave Queen their first *Billboard* chart-topper in 1979, and Mack went on to produce five Queen albums, plus solo offerings from Mercury and Taylor.

Killer performance

Right: Brian has stated that the serrated edge of the coin he uses instead of a standard plectrum may contribute to the instantly recognizable sound he generates from the Red Special. Many aspiring axemen have tried to emulate the distinctive sound and learn May's celebrated licks.

Queen's electrifying stage show made a live album a natural choice, and the European dates early in 1979 – essentially, a continuation of the Jazz tour of America at the back end of '78 – were used to produce a double set. *Live Killers* was a 90-minute romp through a string of the band's big hitters, including "Bohemian Rhapsody" and an acoustic version of "Love of My Life", which was released as a single. It failed to break the Top 50 in the UK, perhaps down to the song's penetration via *A Night at the Opera*. But it went on to give Queen a smash hit in South America, reaching top spot in Brazil and Argentina, and in the latter country remaining in the chart for a year. When performing the song, Freddie would break off and conduct an audience singalong. Even in South America the fans were word perfect, testament to the international language of pop music.

Left: Freddie has a ballet lesson at Covent Garden, London, in 1979.

Studio toys

"There were no limits," said Brian, referring to Queen's approach to studio work and the creative possibilities it offered. Gone were the days when Queen had to record at unearthly hours when bigger names had finished their session. Queen were the big name, a stadium supergroup who could indulge their every whim when they were in recording mode. *A Night at the Opera* had featured "every sound, from a tuba to a comb", as Freddie put it. That was reminiscent of the Beatles raiding the *Abbey Road* cupboards a decade earlier as they pushed the sonic boundaries. The Fab Four were a huge influence on Queen, but, as Brian pointed out, they reaped the benefit of substantial technical advances. "We had better toys than The Beatles had... we were like artists let loose with loads of lovely paint pots."

"I just cook on stage."
Freddie doing what he did better than anyone else at London's Wembley Arena (left) and at the Ernst Merck Halle in Hamburg (opposite) during Queen's European tour, spring 1978. Many will recall the playful call-and-response game he played with the Live Aid audience to establish a rapport. It was something he did regularly during shows, and he was well aware of the power "Freddie the performer" wielded. Away from the spotlight he was much more subdued, but when he was "on" Freddie held vast crowds in the palm of his hand – and he loved it. "That kind of surge is unequalled. The feeling I get from the audience is greater than sex."

At the top of their game

Left and opposite: Performing in Leiden, Holland, November 27, 1980. It was the European leg of The Game tour, promoting Queen's eighth studio album. The first long-player to emerge from the collaboration with producer Reinhold Mack at Musicland Studios in Munich, *The Game* put Queen back on top, following the tepid reception its predecessor, *Jazz*, had received. It yielded four UK Top 20 singles, but in another first for the band, did even better in America. A five-week run at No.1 in the US outstripped its chart showing at home, while "Crazy Little Thing Called Love" and "Another One Bites the Dust" both topped the *Billboard* Hot 100. *The Game* became the only Queen album to reach the top spot on both sides of the Atlantic, an impressive start for Mack, who gets a name-check in "Dragon Attack".

Restricted palette

Receiving a gold disc for "Crazy Little Thing Called Love". Freddie said that knowing only a few guitar chords forced him to work within a limited framework. Brian May knew his way around a fretboard rather better, and was given his head in the solo break, for which, at Reinhold Mack's behest, he swapped his Red Special for a Fender Telecaster. He wasn't keen, but Mack felt the sound of an old Telecaster better suited the period feel of the song. The producer was vindicated by the song's impressive chart performance: No. 2 in the UK and No. 1 in America was the best showing of any Queen single in the two key markets. "Mack," said Freddie, "is an absolute genius."

Star Fleet

Opposite: Brian May, pictured with fellow guitar legend Eddie Van Halen in the early 1980s. At Brian's invitation, the two got together for a jam session in Los Angeles in April 1983, when Queen were taking a break from touring and recording. The scratch pals' band also included Fred Mandel, former Alice Cooper keyboard player who had played on Queen's Hot Space tour; REO Speedwagon drummer Alan Gratzer; and bassist Phil Chen, who had played in Rod Stewart's backing band. The impromptu session spawned the single "Star Fleet", Brian's first solo release. The song, an arrangement of the theme tune to a TV sci-fi programme popular with his son, received little airplay and stalled at No. 65 in the charts. A three-track mini-album, *Star Fleet Project*, followed. Credited to "Brian May and Friends" and including an old May number "Let Me Out", it broke the Top 40 in November 1983. 'Just a little trip out,' said Brian, reassuring those who thought he might be quitting Queen and forming a new supergroup.

Right: Freddie sprouts a bushy moustache, which didn't go down too well with some fans, who showered him with disposable razors. Speaking about his change of image in the early 80s, he said he'd look ridiculous wearing the outfits of the early Queen days, sporting those long, flowing locks and black nail varnish, adding: "I looked ridiculous then, but it worked."

"No synth" rule abandoned

Just as Freddie knew how to have an audience eating out of his hand, Brian, too, was aware of the special power that came with being part of a supergroup that could fill the biggest stadiums. "There is something magical about a quarter of a million people being out there, and knowing that they can hear you properly, and knowing that one little movement of a millimetre of your finger will affect them in some way." On the hugely successful 1980 album *The Game*, guitars were less prominent, and there was an addition to the instrumental line-up: the synthesiser. Queen had made a point of saying their earlier albums were synth-free zones, but with Reinhold Mack in the producer's chair, they were encouraged to expand their musical palette.

Performance indicator

Left and opposite: On stage during Queen's European tour, autumn 1980. With Freddie at the microphone, it could be any song; Freddie hammering out a D chord on 12-string acoustic guitar could mean just one thing: "Crazy little Thing Called Love", which became a fixture in the band's shows right through to 1986 and their concert finale. Freddie might have changed his image, but his views on live performance didn't waver. "People want to be entertained in various ways. One way I know they don't want to be entertained is for people to just come on and play their songs. They can hear it on the record." Queen were all about a wider sensory experience, not just a simulacrum of the studio sound.

Marriage lines

Freddie and John on tour in 1980. John Deacon had his first single success with "You're My Best Friend", the follow-up to "Bohemian Rhapsody" which reached No. 7 in the UK chart in summer 1976. He was the most diffident when it came to presenting his ideas to the band, happy to take a back seat among bigger egos and louder voices. John wrote the song for Veronica Tetzlaff, his college sweetheart whom he married in January 1975, when she was pregnant with the first of their six children. The first band member to leave bachelorhood behind, he took his new responsibilities seriously, seeking money from Trident for a deposit on a family home. The request was flatly refused, Trident bosses sticking to a rigid £60-per-week allowance while they recouped their investment money from the profits now rolling in. It was this mercenary attitude that Freddie attacked so vituperatively in the song "Death on Two Legs", which he said was the most vicious lyric he ever wrote.

Flash soundtrack

By Queen standards, the gap between the release of *Jazz* and *The Game* had been a lengthy one – over a year and a half – the hiatus filled by the live set *Live Killers*. Normal productivity levels were restored as two albums were issued within six months. In December 1980 the *Flash Gordon* soundtrack hit the record shops, giving Queen their ninth UK Top 10 album in six years. They were given carte blanche to provide the score for the lavish space romp, which starred Sam J Jones as the 1930s comic-strip hero. It represented an interesting departure, Brian in particular immersing himself in the project and taking a co-producer credit with Mack. Some fans felt it sat uncomfortably in the Queen canon, and it peaked at No. 23 in the US. But the May-penned single "Flash's Theme" hit the fun, frolicsome spot, matching the album's performance by making the UK Top 10. *Record Mirror* called it "heroic material on a grand scale", with "a resounding pulse beat before Mercury goes into overdrive".

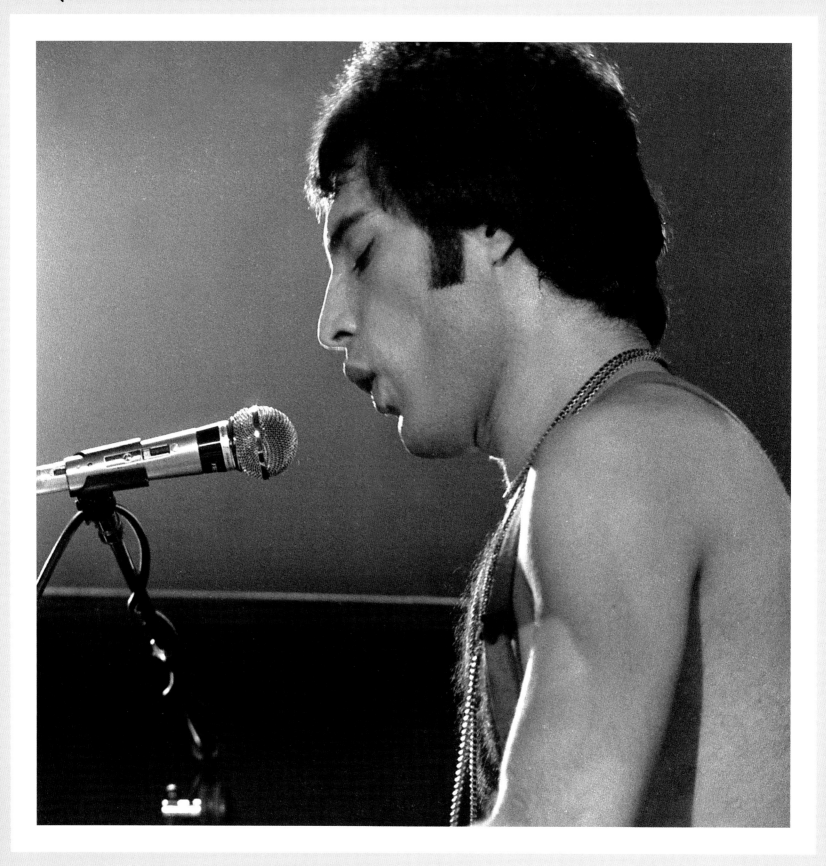

Public affection, private pain

On stage Freddie played to the crowd; off it he played Russian roulette. "Sometimes I wake up in a cold sweat, in fear because I'm alone. That's why I go out looking for someone who will love me, even if it's just for a one-night stand." There were betrayals that created trust issues and made him extremely wary. Freddie was ever wondering whether those drawn to him were primarily attracted to the trappings of success. "Success has brought me millions of pounds and worldwide adulation," Freddie remarked, "but not the thing we all need: a loving relationship."

Another one bites the dust

Opposite: John Deacon's Motown influence can be heard on "Another One Bites the Dust", which made No. 2 in the black American chart as well as topping the Hot 100. Freddie recalled that many fans turned up to see the group that had recorded the song, expecting to see black artists. The fact that Deacon had gone "perhaps more violently black than the rest of us", as Brian May put it, caused a degree of friction during the making of the *Hot Space* album. On Deacon's "Back Chat", one of the album's single releases, May said he had to persuade his band mate to steer the song onto a more "central path, and get a bit of heaviness into it". He won that argument and a guitar solo was added, but even in gutsier form the song didn't match the phenomenal success of "Another One Bites the Dust", barely scraping into the UK Top 40. It wasn't released as a single in America.

Above: If a scrap of paper or piece of merchandise wasn't to hand, Queen fans went to some lengths to get an autograph trophy to take home. Bare flesh wasn't unusual, and Queen parties were renowned for the amount of that on display. In a 2011 interview Taylor said of those wild excesses: "If we could screw that much money out of the record company to have an almighty blowout, then why not?"

Latin examination

Freddie and Brian on stage during the 1980 Jazz tour. Queen had rocked Europe, America, Asia and Oceania, and soon set their sights on just about the only frontier that remained to be conquered. In February 1981 the band embarked on a three-week, seven-date tour of South America; modest by their standards, but a seminal moment in the band's 20-year career. It was a risk; taking Queen on the road was an expensive business, and this was uncharted territory. They needn't have worried, for the reception was staggering. Five shows in Argentina were followed by two at Sao Paulo's Morumbi Stadium, where a 131,000-strong crowd set a new record for a paying audience. The band were blown away by how popular they were, measured by the fans' word-perfect rendition of their songs. Said Freddie: "By the end of it I wanted to buy up the entire continent and install myself as president."

Chapter Three

A Kind of Magic

Relieving pressure

Left and opposite: Freddie giving it his all during the Oakland, California leg of Queen's 1982 Hot Space tour. The album made the Top 5 in the UK, though it was a dance-orientated departure too far for many die-hard fans. Single cuts "Body Language" and "Back Chat" failed to break the Top 20, while "Las Palabras de Amor" stalled at No. 17. Bucking the trend was "Under Pressure", a serendipitous collaboration with David Bowie, who happened to drop by Mountain Studios, Montreux while they were recording. As they began jamming, a song took shape that would give Queen their first UK chart-topper since "Bohemian Rhapsody". According to Roger Taylor, John Deacon came up with the bass riff that underpins the song, only to forget it when they broke for refreshments. Taylor remembered it and saved the day.

Pulling power

Above: Meeting fans during the American leg of the Hot Space tour, summer 1982. For many it would be their last chance to see the band live, for this would be Queen's final US tour. Freddie said Queen was "like a chariot with four horses". During the periods when they joined up they pulled together to productive effect, each taking a turn at the reins. But he also said writing and performing was "a job, like anybody else", and recognized that the time would come when he couldn't disport himself on stage in his habitual way. Untrained for any other kind of work, and horrified at the boredom he would suffer if he retired and lived off his fortune, Freddie anticipated that he would eventually focus on writing and producing, for which age was immaterial.

Mott mate

Above: Freddie and Mott the Hoople frontman Ian Hunter, pictured at a New York party, August 1982. They had been friends since Queen opened for Mott on a UK tour in 1973 and filled the support slot on an American trip the following spring. To seal the initial deal, at a time when Queen's management were keen to raise the band's profile, a £3,000 fee had been paid. This was ostensibly a contribution towards costs, though it has also been seen as "buying" the group onto the tour, a practice that was not unknown. While the shows generated plenty of buzz, it didn't translate to the music press. Amazingly, some thought the band derivative – Led Zeppelin was sometimes cited. They were also criticized for being overhyped. Freddie put the negativity down to the fact that music journos couldn't pigeonhole Queen, and that the band took off without their ringing endorsement. "Many of them decided we needed a good slagging, just because we had the nerve to get to the top before they had given us the say-so."

"minimalist era"

Right: Brian on stage during the European leg of the Hot Space tour. He had recently become a second-time father, but was not one for lengthy sabbaticals, especially when stung by the lukewarm reception accorded Queen's latest album. May's Latin-laced "Las Palabras De Amor" – "The Words of Love" – issued June '82, was the third UK single release from *Hot Space*, and though it outperformed its predecessor, "Body Language", by Queen's standards it was a relative failure. Brian defended what he called the band's "minimalist era", which caused such a division of opinion among fans. But "Las Palabras De Amor", he said, "was un-minimalist... really rather romantic," adding, "I like the track, painted with a very light brush." To give the song a welcome boost at home – it wasn't released as a single in America – Queen made their first appearance on *Top of the Pops* since performing "Good Old Fashioned Lover Boy" on the show in 1977.

Opposite: Freddy pictured on the Hot Space tour.

Staying trim

Freddie succumbs to a little light grooming in 1982, keeping in trim for yet another exhaustive year of touring that saw Queen take the Hot Space show around Europe and North America. Freddie ran behind Roger Taylor and Brian May in terms of venturing into the solo arena. Not until the mid-80s would he finally step outside the familial band unit on disc. It wasn't a major departure, for even when working on Queen albums they effectively operated individually, "like four little solo projects working side by side". Fans inevitably wondered whether the extramural activities signalled the end of the band, something Freddie waved away as he approached his 40th birthday in the middle of the decade. "Queen will always carry on in our same extreme, crazy, confident manner," he'd said when Queen were breaking into the big time, and that held true even when temporarily they went their own artistic ways.

A love of ballet

Opposite: Dancer Wayne Sleep
takes the supporting role as
Freddie attends a London
party for *42nd Street*, August
1984. Sleep had trained with
The Royal Ballet, with whom
Freddie had performed in
1979. As someone who set
so much store in his own
sphere on theatricality, graceful
movement and the whole
visual experience, Freddie had
an abiding love for ballet and
would try to slip unnoticed into
theatres to watch productions
when commitments permitted.
Mikhail Baryshnikov in particular
left him playing the awestruck
fan for once.

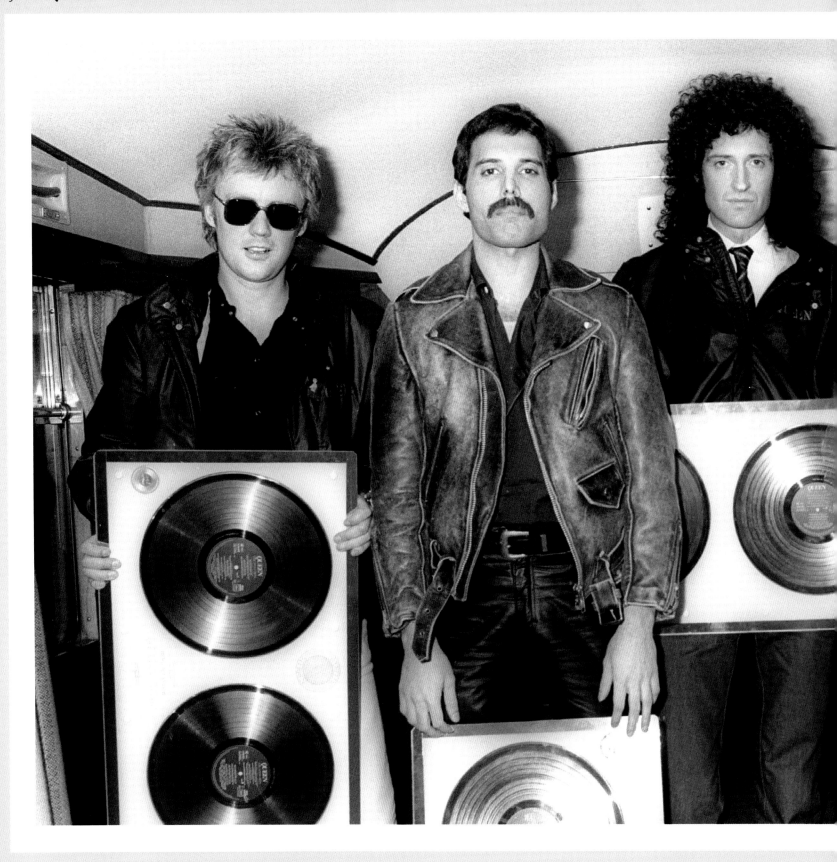

Going Dutch

Adding to the trophy haul with a gold disc for the 1981 *Greatest Hits* album, which would go on to smash the UK long-player sales record and top charts around the world. The band are pictured showing off their gold award in the Netherlands, where Queen were enormously popular. "Somebody to Love", "Crazy Little Thing Called Love", "Radio Ga Ga" and "I Want to Break Free" all reached the top of the Dutch charts – outperforming the home market – and eight Queen albums would also hit the No. 1 spot in that country. Dutch fans joined the party slightly belatedly: neither of the band's first two albums made the listings, and the singles "Keep Yourself Alive" and "Seven Seas of Rhye" also fell by the wayside. Queenmania took off there in autumn 1974 with the release of *Sheer Heart Attack* and "Killer Queen".

Hit parade

Queen's first *Greatest Hits* compilation included all the biggie 45s over a seven-year period, from "Seven Seas of Rhye" to "Flash". The latter song had been issued as a single just a year before the album's November 1981 release. So determined were the band to saturate the record only with their top sellers that "Tie Your Mother Down", a gig favourite guaranteed to bring the house down, failed to make the cut having peaked just outside the UK Top 30. "Love of My Life" and "Spread Your Wings" were omitted for the same reason. It proved a winning formula, the album going on to become the biggest-selling UK long-player of all time. Aggregating the multiple re-entries, the album has spent over eight years in the UK listings, with sales approaching the six million mark. Track selections were altered to suit overseas markets. In the US, for example, "Under Pressure" and "Keep Yourself Alive" were included, neither of which featured in the UK release. The hits package went platinum eight times over in the States, and worldwide sales tip the scales at a hefty 25 million.

The full works

Opposite: Freddie performing at Wembley Arena, one of four dates Queen played there in September 1984 during the Works tour. The album marked a scorching return to form following the rumblings of discontent surrounding *Hot Space*. By the time the band headed to London for the first of those Wembley dates, they had seen "Radio Ga Ga", "I Want To Break Free" and "It's A Hard Life" all make the UK Top 10, with Brian's "Hammer To Fall" about to give them a fourth hit from the same parental source. The Works just missed out on becoming Queen's fourth UK chart-topping studio album, peaking at No. 2. It didn't fare quite so well in America. This "royal feast of hard rock", as *Rolling Stone* dubbed it, stalled just outside the Top 20. The fact that the cross-dressing joke of the "I Want To Break Free" video fell flat in some parts of the States, particularly the Bible Belt, was one contributory factor. Another was the fallout from corruption allegations concerning the murky world of record promotion, a scandal in which the band's new US distributor, Capitol, became embroiled. With no American concerts to galvanize interest, *The Works* struggled to gain traction in that country.

Left: Freddie on stage at Madison Square Garden, July 27, 1982. Never interested in the idea of "bashing the drums at the back", Freddie was also quick to distinguish between lead singer and leader. It was widely assumed that Freddie's was the biggest ego, that his temperamental outbursts would have been the source of much discord. Brian May said that he was actually the chief peacemaker when the fur began to fly.

Breaking free

John Deacon's "I Want to Break Free" was a monster worldwide hit, a worthy single successor to Roger's "Radio Ga Ga", which it trailed by a whisker in the UK chart, peaking at No. 3. British audiences lapped up the larky video, but the joke didn't translate happily to the international arena. In Latin America, where it was seen as an anthem championing liberty, the sight of Freddie in false breasts didn't play well. Middle America was also affronted at the sight of rock stars camping it up in drag. MTV refused it airtime, and the single failed to break the Top 40 on the *Billboard* Hot 100. The band suffered a dip in fortune as far as the American market was concerned. The video conceit seems like classic Mercury; it actually came from Roger Taylor, who made a rather fetching, gum-chewing St Trinians-type schoolgirl.

Collaborative effort

In a departure from normal creative practice, Freddie and Brian collaborated on "Is This the World We Created...?", the end track on *The Works*. Having identified that the album needed "one of those little acoustic things", as Freddie called it – a song with the same feel as "Love of My Life" – the two decided on an impromptu writing session instead of coming up with separate ideas. Scarcely two minutes long, the song might have remained a lesser known item in Queen's extensive canon had it not featured in Live Aid the following summer. Its self-reproachful, conscience-pricking theme, inviting mankind to take a long, hard look at itself, was a perfect foil for the party spirit of the "global jukebox". After tearing up Wembley Stadium with their main set, Freddie and Brian returned at dusk to instil an apposite reflective mood with their duet.

Currency of the world

Freddie, pictured with John Deacon, belts out one of Queen's anthems at Wembley in September 1984. Queen's great anthems, such as "We Are the Champions" and "We Will Rock You" were "the currency of the world", said Brian May. That contention was borne out when the former song featured in an episode of *The Simpsons*, a show famed for its pop culture references. The band's fan base was certainly worldwide, and after conquering South America they even contemplated taking the roadshow to Russia and China. Brian emphasized the importance of giving each band member his creative head, as failure to do so, he believed, was a common cause of rifts and splits in groups. Avoiding that pitfall, along with spending time apart in between touring and recording, kept the band energised and sustained them as a creative force for 20 years.

Hits all round

Montreux, May 12, 1984. Queen play the televised Golden Rose Pop Festival, their mimed set comprising four songs from *The Works*, including the Taylor-penned lead single "Radio Ga Ga". Roger credited his son Felix with the title of his paean to the humble transistor in the all-pervasive video age. A child's lavatorial throwaway remark – "radio ca-ca" – became one of Queen's best loved songs, reaching UK No. 2 (kept off top spot by Frankie Goes to Hollywood's "Relax"). It represented yet another milestone in the band's career as all four had now written songs that had made the top five in one of the big two markets, America and the UK. There was no shortage of irony in the fact that a song that bemoaned the supplanting of radio by video – "We hardly need to use our ears" – itself became an MTV favourite, featuring scenes from Fritz Lang's 1927 sci-fi classic *Metropolis*.

Heading

Above: Divided by sexuality, united spiritually. "We'll probably grow old together," said Freddie of Mary Austin, but had to accept that she, too, would pursue other relationships. Mary's lovers included Jo Burt, bass player with the Tom Robinson Band and, later, Black Sabbath. There was clearly no ill feeling on Freddie's part: Burt played on his 1985 debut solo album *Mr Bad Guy*.

Opposite: Freddie sports the military look as he plays groom to actress Jane Seymour at Fashion Aid, staged at London's Royal Albert Hall, November 5, 1985. Seymour looked stunning in a dress designed by David and Elizabeth Emmanuel, creators of Princess Diana's wedding gown four years earlier. Outfits by some of the biggest names in fashion, such as Calvin Klein and Yves St Laurent, were on view. Michael and Shakira Caine were among the glitterati in attendance. But Freddie was the big draw, and he milked the moment, tossing flowers from his "bride's" bouquet into the audience.

Live Aid

Wembley Stadium, July 13, 1985. Queen steal the Live Aid show, with Freddie at his strutting best. Roger Taylor admitted that at that time the band were "in a bit of a trough" after a decade at the top. Their standing had also been dented by the decision to play Sun City the previous year, which attracted considerable opprobrium. Queen, who hadn't featured on the Band Aid single, weren't taking any chances when there was a 70,000-strong audience to be entertained, not to mention an estimated two billion watching on television. They warmed up for the worldwide, consciousness-raising party by rehearsing exhaustively, ensuring they were primed and ready to pack as many hits as possible into their 18-minute slot. They rocked the world with bravura renditions of "Bohemian Rhapsody", "Radio GaGa", "Hammer to Fall", "Crazy Little Thing Called Love", "We Will Rock You" and "We are the Champions". Freddie even found time for some call-and-response playfulness that the audience lapped up. It was "a fascinating kind of power," said Paul Gambaccini, a DJ with an encyclopedic knowledge of the music business.

This is extraordinary

The Live Aid bill was a veritable Who's Who of rock and pop, but all played second fiddle to Queen that day. "Best thing there," said Francis Rossi, who opened the show with Status Quo. He then added a playful expletive expressing mock envy. Elton John matched those sentiments. Spandau Ballet lead singer Tony Hadley watched boggle-eyed as Freddie orchestrated the hand-clapping on "Radio GaGa" and said he wished his band had a song like that. And Bob Geldof, the man who had put the "global jukebox" on, stopped in his tracks backstage when he heard Queen and the reaction they were eliciting. 'This is extraordinary,' he said of the spine-tingling performance that gave him plenty of ammunition when it came to facing the cameras and inviting those watching to dig deep into their pockets.

Mr Bad Guy

Queen pictured in 1985, when they had every reason to look pleased with life. Sales of their back catalogue rocketed on the back of the Live Aid tour de force. Freddie also released his long awaited debut solo album in April that year. Some of the songs on *Mr Bad Guy* were Queen session leftovers. Freddie had already had his first UK Top 10 hit away from the band with one such number, "Love Kills", which featured in Giorgio Moroder's reworking of Fritz Lang's 1927 silent classic *Metropolis*. "There Must Be More to Life Than This" and "Man Made Paradise", both off the new album, were other songs originally up for consideration on Queen long-players. *Mr Bad Guy* made a respectable No. 6 in the UK chart, and the lead single, "I Was Born to Love You", peaked just outside the Top 10. The follow-up, "Made in Heaven" was an early contender for the title of the long-player before Freddie had a change of heart. A decade later, the song would appear in revamped form on Queen's 15th and final studio album, and this time, four years on from Freddie's death, it did take the titular honours.

Group dynamic

Like Roger and Brian's solo offerings, Freddie's *Mr Bad Guy* failed to reach the dizzy heights of many Queen recordings. "One Vision", released in November 1985 and the band's first single in almost a year, demonstrated yet again the group's ensemble power. The main writing credit went to Taylor, who was incensed at press accusations that the plea for global fellowship enshrined in the lyric was an attempt to ride the Live Aid wave. The inspiration, he said, came from the words of Martin Luther King, whose "I have a dream" speech is referenced in the song. "One Vision" was a solid UK Top 10 hit, as was the next single, Roger's "A Kind of Magic", issued early in the new year. Both songs appeared on the 1986 album of the same name, and both were in the set list of the accompanying Magic tour. American resistance remained, however. Neither "One Vision" nor "A Kind of Magic" broke the Top 40 on the *Billboard* chart.

Final magical flourish

Above: Queen's final tour gets underway in Stockholm, June 7, 1986. The band were at the top of their game as they criss-crossed Europe, grossing £13 million as they signed off in a glorious two-month-long valediction. *A Kind of Magic* – which also furnished the movie *Highlander* with its soundtrack– had given them their first UK chart-topping album since *The Game* six years earlier. There was a triumphant return to Wembley Stadium, which they had rocked to the foundations at Live Aid, and a memorable concert at Budapest's Népstadion, Queen's sole Hungarian sojourn. Was Freddie, about to turn 40, simply slowing down and tiring of all the globetrotting? Was the partying beginning to pall? It has even been suggested that he already had an inkling of the disease that would eventually ravage his body.

Opposite: August 9, 1986: The band arrive by helicopter at Knebworth Park, near London, for what will be their final live appearance. Freddie said touring exacted a heavy physical toll – the equivalent of running back-to-back marathons. Even so, Brian May said the frontman's pained grumblings at the end of the Magic tour were no different from previous complaints about the rigours of life on the road, and it wasn't clear at the time that this was to be their last hurrah as a live band.

"I'd had enough"

Left and opposite: Freddie lights
up the stage for the last time at
Knebworth, which had been added
to the Magic tour itinerary due to
colossal demand. "I'd had enough of
those bombastic lights and staging
effects. I didn't think at my age that
I should be running around in a
leotard any more."

Time pieces

Above: July 12, 1986: With the Magic tour in full swing, Freddie duets with glamour model Samantha Fox at the post-Wembley party. It was a raucous affair in the best traditions of the band who let their hair down like no other. Celebrity guests included Cliff Richard, star of the musical *Time*, for which Freddie had recorded a couple of songs. The show's writer-producer was Mercury's close friend Dave Clark, who made his own mark on the pop charts fronting the Dave Clark Five. Freddie released *Time*'s title song as a single, coinciding with the musical's London premiere in April '86. It reached No. 32 in the UK chart.

Opposite: May 1986: Relaxing on the terrace of Montreux Palace Hotel as the band prepare for another appearance at the Swiss resort's famed Golden Rose Pop Festival. Freddie fell in love with the municipality when Queen first recorded at its Mountain Studios facility, which the band subsequently acquired. Sitting between Lake Geneva and the Alps, Montreux was one of the singer's favourite boltholes. A decade after this photograph was taken, a statue immortalising Freddie would be unveiled there.

He who wears the crown

Left: Freddie, crowned and regally robed at Wembley Stadium, where Queen played two shows, July 11 and 12, 1986. Unbeknown to fans, the band were entering the final stretch of their performing career, but many recording triumphs, both individual and group, still lay ahead. As the Magic tour wound down, Queen issued the May-penned single "Who Wants to Live Forever", another cut from the *Highlander* soundtrack. The song spoke of a man coming to terms with immortality, and the pain it brings as he sees his loved one age and die. Brian was deeply affected by the loss of his father and the break-up of his marriage, which occurred in rapid succession, though the haunting lyrics also foreshadow events surrounding his band mate. Freddie's modus vivendi had been to pack in as much fun as possible during his allotted time on earth; it was quality of life that counted, not quantity.

Opposite: Another change of image for rock's great chameleon as Freddie dons formal attire. He sported a white-tie dress suit in the video accompanying "Who Wants to Live Forever", and was similarly decked out when he took to the stage with operatic diva Montserrat Caballé as they duetted in celebration of the Barcelona '92 Olympic Games. Regardless of costume, Freddie's performance credo remained the same. "If I'm seen to be having fun on stage, I think it comes across."

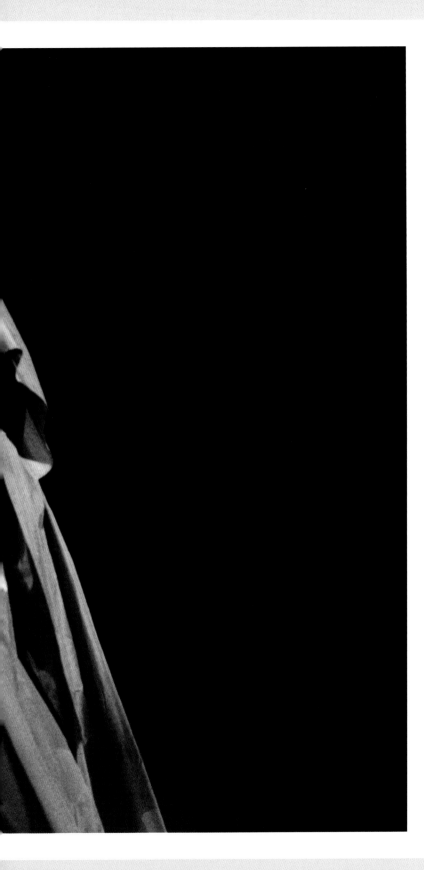

Taking the Olympic stage

Freddie jumped at the opportunity to perform with Spanish soprano Montserrat Caballé, whom he greatly admired. With Mike Moran he co-wrote "Barcelona" – the diva's home city – which they performed at the Ku Club, Ibiza, May 29, 1987, in a TV special celebrating the award of the 1992 Olympic Games to the Catalan city. Released as a single in October, it hit No. 8 in the UK chart, and topped that five years later – reaching No. 2 – when the Games were in full flow. Mercury also took to the stage with Caballé at Barcelona's La Nit open-air festival, October 8, 1988 – the official launchpad for the Olympic sporting spectacular – in a lip-synced performance of the song that became the city's anthem. It was to be Freddie's final live appearance. The physical manifestations of his disease had begun to show, disguised for the cameras by the use of heavy make-up. Those in close proximity knew his protestations to the world that all was well were far wide of the mark, and rumours had already begun circulating in the media.

Brian and the soap queen

Opposite: Brian and actress Anita Dobson became an item after they met at a film premiere in 1986 and he invited her to Queen's Wembley show during the Magic tour. Dobson's fame matched May's in the mid-80s as she starred in the enormously popular soap opera EastEnders, playing feisty landlady and emotionally bruised wife Angie Watts. Anita had a UK Top 10 hit with the May-produced "Anyone Can Fall in Love", sung to the EastEnders theme tune, and he also handed her one of his songs left over from the *Works* sessions – "Let Me In (Your Heart Again)" – which featured on her 1988 album, *Talking of Love*. Brian also wrote the title track, her second single release. It wasn't all one-way traffic: he credited Anita with the throwaway comment on burning ambition that fired him to write "I Want It All", which brought Queen their biggest hit for three years when it reached UK No. 3 in May 1989. The couple married in 2000.

Left: Freddie and Annie Lennox strike a pose at the 1987 Ivor Novello Awards ceremony, held at London's Grosvenor House Hotel, where Queen had the Outstanding Contribution to British Music laurels conferred upon them. Five years later, Lennox would take Mercury's place – vocally speaking – when she teamed up with David Bowie to perform "Under Pressure" at the singer's Wembley tribute concert.

Sabbath pals

Left and opposite: July 1989: Brian May joins his close friend and fellow axe hero, Black Sabbath's Tommy Iommi, to record a version of "Smoke on the Water", part of the Armenian earthquake appeal. An album fund-raiser followed a year later, the set list including Black Sabbath's "Headless Cross", the title track from their 1989 long-player, on which Brian guested. May was also good friends with veteran drummer Cozy Powell, formerly with Rainbow and ELP and who made his Sabbath debut on the same album. The two recorded and performed together extensively when Brian branched out on his own in the 1990s, after Freddie's death. Powell had just finished working on May's 1998 album *Another World* when he was killed in an automobile accident.

The Cross

Roger Taylor and model Deborah Leng – best known for her suggestive devouring of a Cadbury's Flake in a TV advertisement – became an item in 1987 and had three children over the next 13 years. When they first got together, there was no Queen project on the horizon so Taylor formed his own band, The Cross, who released three albums over the next five years. He left his drum stool to combine guitar work with lead vocals in the band, which enjoyed a degree of success in Germany but made little impression in the major UK and American markets. The Cross's debut album, *Shove It*, did feature the track "Heaven For Everyone", with Freddie guesting on vocals. It received rather more exposure when it appeared on the Queen album *Made in Heaven*, issued four years after Freddie's death.

Opposite: Freddie accompanied by Mary Austin.

Marking an anniversary

Opposite: February 1990: Freddie attends Queen's 20th anniversary party at London's Groucho Club – a neat choice of venue given Queen's nod to the Marx Brothers in two mid-70s albums. Perhaps Freddie feared he wouldn't live to see February '91, when John Deacon passed the 20-year mark as a member of the band. His altered appearance attracted much press speculation, countered with robust rebuttals. Freddie's two-pronged response to a febrile rumour mill was to stay out of the spotlight as much as possible and work. The anniversary party was one of the last times he was photographed in public. Freddie retreated for long periods to Montreux, away from the prying eyes of a hack pack that scented a major story.

Left: Freddie with Catherine Zeta-Jones and Jill Gascoine at a party for the new cast of the musical *42nd Street*.

Solo effort

Brian May, pictured during a sound check for the Guitar Legends concert staged in Seville, Spain, October 1991. May helped organize the festival, which featured such legendary names as B B King and Les Paul, along with latter-day guitar heroes including Steve Vai and Joe Satriani. Also on the bill was ex-Free and Bad Company vocalist Paul Rodgers, who a decade later would go on the road with May and Roger Taylor.

Freddie Mercury was desperately ill by the time the concert took place, with only a month left to live. Even so, he encouraged May to put his solo career first, insisting the latter press ahead with the scheduled release of his new single "Driven By You". His death, said Freddie, could only boost sales. The song, which adorned an advertisement for the Ford Motor Company, and which he performed at the Guitar Legends concert, made the UK Top 10, and also walked off with an Ivor Novello award in the TV/Radio Commercial category.

Chapter Four

The Show Must Go On

"Biggest send-off in history"

Guns 'n' Roses guitarist Slash joins Brian on stage at the Freddie Mercury Tribute Concert, held at Wembley Stadium, April 20, 1992. At Freddie's passing the group had issued a statement mourning the loss of "the greatest and most beloved member of our family". It referred to the "magical times" they had shared, and looked forward to staging an event "to celebrate his life in the style to which he was accustomed". The resulting concert, promoting Aids awareness to a worldwide audience as well as paying homage to a rock legend, featured a galaxy of stars performing Queen songs. Slash and Def Leppard's Joe Elliott joined the band for a roof-raising rendition of "Tie Your Mother Down", which by itself fulfilled the aim enshrined in Brian's introductory words: "We're going to give him the biggest send-off in history!"

Stars come out for Freddie

Left and opposite: At the top
of the Wembley show all three
surviving band members made
moving, uplifting remarks.
After Brian said they were
here "to celebrate the life
and work and dreams of one
Freddie Mercury", Roger Taylor
addressed the 72,000 people
present and a global audience
with the words: "Today is for
Freddie, it's for you, it's to tell
everybody around the world
that Aids affects us all. That's
what these red ribbons are all
about. You can cry as much as
you like." John Deacon thanked
the stellar artist line-up who had
"given their time and energy
to make this tribute to Freddie
a reality". They included David
Bowie and Annie Lennox, who
duetted on "Under Pressure";
Lisa Stansfield and George
Michael, performing "I Want
To Break Free" and "Somebody
to Love" respectively, as well
as uniting for "These Are The
Days of Our Lives"; Black
Sabbath's Tommy Iommi and
Roger Daltrey, who teamed
up in a rendition of "I Want
It All"; Robert Plant, tackling
"Crazy Little Thing Called Love";
and Elton John, who took on
"Bohemian Rhapsody", with
help from Axl Rose.

"Goodnight, Freddie, we love you"

Freddie Mercury was a huge fan of Liza
Minnelli, and she was given the honour
of leading the grand finale at the singer's
tribute concert, hitting the high notes in "We
Are the Champions" before being joined on
stage by the other artists. But for many the
most moving moment of the show came
when Brian May swapped his guitar for the
keyboard to perform a song he introduced
as having been written some time before
but which "had never seen the light of
day". He added: "My excuse for singing
it, I think, is that it's the best thing that I
have to offer." The song, "Too Much Love
Will Kill You", would be issued as a May
solo single, and four years later it would
chart once again under the Queen banner,
using Mercury's vocals from the original
recording. Meanwhile, it was left to Roger to
close the tribute concert proceedings with
the simple message: "Goodnight, Freddie,
we love you."

Hall of Fame

"Queen took rock 'n' roll to places it had never been before ...to this day no band has come close to Queen's magnificent command of rock's pomp and circumstance." With those words Queen were inducted into the Rock 'n' Roll Hall of Fame in March 2001, Dave Grohl and Taylor Hawkins of the Foo Fighters providing the laudatory introductions at the New York ceremony before Brian May and Roger Taylor took their acceptance bows. "It means more than all the Grammys we never got," quipped Roger, while Brian expressed his gratitude "to the people of America for taking us to your hearts over the last 30 years". The applause was ratcheted up still further as Freddie's mother, Jer, joined them on stage to accept the award on her son's behalf. Brian and Roger then joined the Foo Fighters duo in a searing performance of "Tie Your Mother Down".

Back to the Light

Left: May and fellow guitar hero George Harrison in 1992. "Things like *The White Album* were religious texts for us, in terms of how free and creative you can be," said May of the Beatles' influence. But while the Beatles' latter days were marked by combustible tensions that culminated in an acrimonious split, Queen managed their internal divisions for two decades in what was, according to Brian, a "perfect creative hothouse". With Freddie gone and the band in limbo, he threw himself into completing his long awaited solo album, *Back to the Light*, released September 1992. The title refers to his recovery from depression; he had been laid low by the collapse of his marriage and death of his father, as well as the loss of his band mate and close friend.

Opposite: Brian May and Mary Austin, pictured at a charity event in November 2002. Austin was the chief beneficiary of Freddie's will, her inheritance including the Kensington mansion he shared with his partner of seven years, Jim Hutton. When it came to handing out bequests, Freddie favoured the most important female figure in his life over the most significant male relationship. The eviction caused much ill feeling. Hutton, who was presented as one of Mercury's household staff to spare family feelings, was also diagnosed HIV positive, but it was lung cancer that claimed his life in 2010.

Shy and retiring

Above and opposite: Brian May and Roger Taylor performing at Hollywood's Club 1650, October 2002. The gig followed the band's being honoured with a star on Hollywood's Walk of Fame, Patti Russo and Steve Vai among those who guested as they tore through a selection of Queen's greatest hits. It was one of numerous awards conferred on the band – just a few months later they would be inducted into the Songwriters Hall of Fame. These accolades and performances took place without John Deacon, who retired from the music scene in 1997. He became something of a reclusive figure after leaving the stage, confining his dealings with his former band mates to business matters and showing not the least inclination to return to the limelight.

Toga party

Right: The timelessness of "We Will Rock You" is put to the test as a Pepsi ad uses it for a commercial set in Ancient Rome. Britney Spears – pictured with toga-clad Taylor and May – and fellow gladiators Beyoncé and Pink refuse to do the imperial bidding of Enrique Iglesias in the Colosseum arena. The crowd, including Roger and Brian, seen fleetingly, rise to the beat and nasty Emperor Enrique ends up facing a peckish lion. "No acting was required," said Roger, which is a good job." Brian added: "It was incredible to work with the three of them, and hear the song come to life in a new way. Freddie would have loved it."

Opposite Brian and Roger pose with their star on the Hollywood Walk of Fame in October 2002.

Phoenix rising

Cape Town, November 29, 2003: Brian duets with Andrea Corr at the 46664 Concert, staged at Green Point Stadium. This Aids awareness event was hosted by Nelson Mandela – the five-digit sequence refers to his prisoner number during his incarceration on Robben Island – part of the former South African president's crusade against a disease that is rife in Africa. May and The Corrs lead singer performed "Is This the World We Created", while Roger Taylor joined Andrea and the rest of her sibling band on their version of the Irish folk tune "Toss the Feathers". Queen music featured prominently. The Soweto Gospel Choir put their stamp on "Bohemian Rhapsody", while Zucchero delivered "I Want It All". The band also appeared on the bill of the 46664 Concert of 2005, with Paul Rodgers on vocals, and their ongoing support for a cause close to their heart can also be seen in the work of the Mercury Phoenix Trust, founded to distribute monies raised from the 1992 tribute concert to Freddie.

Song for the innocent

Left: Brian accompanies Anastacia at the 46664 Concert in 2003. The American singer performed "We Will Rock You" and "We Are the Champions", and also joined an ad hoc supergroup consisting of Queen, half of U2 and ex-Eurythmics Dave Stewart in a rendition of "Amandla". May co-wrote this stirring anthem, whose dedication is enshrined in the lyric: "This song is for the innocent / Who never had a youth".

Opposite: Roger and Brian on stage at Green Point with Dave Stewart, the chief architect in turning Nelson Mandela's vision into a reality. The Queen duo helped organize the event, and the three stars joined forces on a new song written by Roger, "Say It's Not True", which was released as a single on December 1, 2007 to mark World Aids Day.

Rebellion on Planet Mall

March 26, 2002: May and Taylor celebrate
the launch of the musical *We Will Rock You* at
London's Dominion Theatre. Pictured left is
the show's writer, Ben Elton, while producer
Robert de Niro gets his hands on the Red
Special. The story is set in a bleak, computer-
led futurescape where music has a prescribed
uniformity, individual expression is suppressed
and instruments are banned. Cue a mighty
rebellion of kids who want to rock out and won't
put up with the bland musical offerings on
Planet Mall any longer. And cue a smorgasbord
of Queen hits. Brian May co-produced the show,
which premiered on May 14, 2002. Not all the
reviews were positive, but it went down a storm
with fans, something reminiscent of Queen's
own career. As well as notching well over 3,000
performances – and counting – in London, the
show has been taken round the world, to places
as far afield as Johannesburg, Tokyo, Las Vegas
and Moscow.

Brian backs Kerry

Opposite and right: May and Taylor performing at the opening-night party for *We Will Rock You*. Pictured with Brian is Kerry Ellis, star of a string of hit stage shows who took the role of Meat in the original production of *We Will Rock You*. One of her numbers was "No One But You", written by May and released as a Queen single in 1998. It is the only song from the post-Freddie era to feature in the show. "No One But You" appeared on Ellis's 2008 three-cut EP *Wicked in Rock*, co-produced by May, and the collaboration continued with her debut album *Anthems*, a chart hit in 2010. Brian backed Ellis on a UK tour the following year.

"Part of the wallpaper"

Brian giving it plenty with the cast of *We Will Rock You* in Las Vegas, December 2004. Apart from providing the title for the phenomenally successful stage show, the song itself also registered yet another landmark in the Queen story. When British boy band Five took "We Will Rock You" to the top of the UK chart in 2000, it meant Queen had registered a home No. 1 in each decade since the 1970s, the first act to achieve that feat. The performance video for the "Five + Queen" version of the song had giant images of Brian and Roger projected onto the sides of buildings. Speaking in 2011, when Queen were inducted into the Q Hall of Fame, Brian said it's great that the band's music has spanned the generations, or, as Roger put it, that Queen had become "part of the wallpaper".

Party at the Palace

The celebrations for Queen Elizabeth II's Golden Jubilee in 2002 included a concert staged in the grounds of Buckingham Palace on June 3. The party got off to a bang with Brian May's stunning rooftop rendition of the National Anthem (opposite), a fixture for so long in Queen's set list. Brian also joined Cliff Richard and S Club 7 on stage (above) for a sensational performance of Cliff's 1958 hit "Move It", the singer stepping aside midstream as May launched into a typically dazzling solo. For their own spot, Brian and Roger performed "Radio Ga Ga" and "We Will Rock You", sharing the vocals before handing the reins to Will Young on "We Are the Champions" and the cast of the *We Will Rock You* stage show for "Bohemian Rhapsody". Queen also backed Phil Collins and Joe Cocker during the show, as well as joining in an all-star, McCartney-led, Beatles-double finale, "All You Need is Love" and "Hey Jude".

A solid gold performance

London, 12 August 2012: Queen show once again they are the go-to band for the big occasion as they rock the Olympic stadium to its foundations during the Games' closing ceremony. Freddie was there in spirit, delivering his trademark call-and-response routine on a giant screen, holding the audience in the palm of his hand, just as he had when the footage was shot at Wembley in 1986. Next up came a scorching rendition of May's "Brighton Rock", after which Brian and Roger backed diva Jessie J in a version of their copper-bottomed crowd-pleaser "We Will Rock You". The show took place a week before Brian turned 65, with Roger just a couple of years away from that landmark. But virtuosity trumps age every time, and the Queen men remain as in-demand as ever. One request that received a positive response came from superstar Lady Gaga, a die-hard Queen fan who took her stage name from one of the band's biggest hits. She admitted to being overwhelmed when May agreed to play on her 2011 album *Born This Way*. For his part, Brian shows no sign of slowing down or contemplating retirement. An indefatigable campaigner for animal welfare who launched the Save Me organization and turned his Surrey estate into a wildlife sanctuary, May says, "When I'm gone, people will no doubt remember me for Queen, but I would much rather be remembered for attempting to change the way we treat our fellow creatures." Fans need have no fear that the Red Special will be a museum piece anytime soon, for the legendary axeman added: "As long as I have fingers that move at all I'll be playing the guitar."

Chronology & Discography

CHRONOLOGY

1946

September 5: Birth of Farrokh Bulsara in Zanzibar.

1947

July 19: Birth of Brian May in Feltham, Middlesex, England.

1949

July 26: Birth of Roger Taylor in Kings Lynn, East Anglia. The family later relocates to Truro, Cornwall.

1951

August 19: Birth of John Deacon in Leicester, England

1955

Farrokh attends St Peter's School, Panchgani, India, where he becomes known as Freddie.

1963

With his father Harold's help, Brian builds the electric guitar that will underpin Queen's sound. Construction of the "Red Special" will take over a year.

Freddie returns to Zanzibar, attending St Joseph's Convent School.

1964

1984, a band that includes Brian May and schoolfriend Tim Staffell, make their debut.

The Bulsara family arrives in Britain, setting up home in Feltham, Middlesex. The Mays live nearby but Freddie and Brian do not meet.

1965

Brian begins a physics and astronomy course at London's Imperial College of Science and Technology.

1966

Freddie begins a graphic art and design course at Ealing College of Art, where Tim Staffell is a fellow student.

1967

May 13: 1984 support Jimi Hendrix at London's Imperial College.

October: Roger Taylor arrives in London to begin a dentistry course at London Hospital Medical School, having made his name as one of Cornwall's top drummers.

December 22: 1984 play a charity show at the London Olympia, the bill including Pink Floyd, The Who and Hendrix.

1968

Brian quits 1984 to focus on his studies. Staffell leaves soon after and the two decide to form a new band, Smile.

Dentistry student Roger Taylor joins Smile after responding to an advertisement on Imperial College's notice board.

October 24: Brian graduates with a BSc (Hons) from Imperial College and embarks on his PhD studies.

October 26: Smile make their debut supporting Pink Floyd at Imperial College.

1969

February 27: Smile perform at London's Albert Hall on a bill that includes Free.

April: Following an approach by Lou Reizner, Smile sign a one-record deal with Mercury Records. A recording session at Trident Studios yields the single "Earth"/"Step On Me". Released in America in August, it makes no impact.

Freddie graduates from Ealing College of Art. He becomes singer with the band Ibex, which morphs into Wreckage. Through Staffell he also becomes part of Smile's circle. Also meets Mary Austin, an enduring presence for the remainder of his life.

October: John Deacon begins studying for an electronics degree at Chelsea College of Technology, part of University of London. An accomplished guitarist, he has played extensively on the Leicester circuit.

1970

Following the demise of Wreckage and a brief stint with Sour Milk Sea, Freddie joins Smile as replacement for the departed Staffell.

Mercury Records drops the band.

Freddie rebrands the group as Queen and changes his surname to Mercury.

June 27: The new band make their debut at Truro City Hall, though they are still billed as Smile.

1971

February: After several bass players come and go, John Deacon joins Queen, completing the line-up that will endure for 20 years.

Queen are invited to test the new De Lane Lea Studio, Wembley, London, producing high-quality demos of "Liar", "Keep Yourself Alive", "The Night Comes Down" and "Jesus".

While working on his doctorate, Brian takes a short-lived teaching job at Stockwell Manor Comprehensive School, Brixton.

1972

Queen reject an offer from Chrysalis Records.

Roger gains a degree in biology, having abandoned his dentistry studies.

John completes his electronics degree.

November: Queen sign a contract with Trident Audio Productions.

1973

February 15: Queen feature on BBC Radio 1 show *Sounds of the Seventies*.

March: EMI sign Queen to a record deal covering the UK and Europe. A US contract with Elektra follows.

July: Release of debut single "Keep Yourself Alive"/"Son and Daughter", which flops after receiving little airplay. Eponymous debut album receives lukewarm reviews, but a white-label copy impresses the makers of *The Old Grey Whistle Test*, which features "Keep Yourself Alive" without knowing the name of the band.

November 12: Queen support Mott the Hoople on a UK tour.

1974

21 February: Queen make their *Top of the Pops* debut, performing "Seven Seas of Rhye", which reaches No.10 in the UK.

March: The band embark on their first headlining tour of the UK. *Queen II* released.

April: First tour of America, supporting Mott the Hoople, truncated when Brian contracts hepatitis.

October: Release of "Killer Queen", which hits No.2 in the UK chart.

November: Release of the album *Sheer Heart Attack*, which also reaches the No.2 spot.

1975

January 18: John marries Veronica Tetzlaff.

February: Queen's first headlining US tour begins.

August: Contract with Trident terminated.

October: Release of "Bohemian Rhapsody", which tops the UK chart for nine weeks. Parent album *A Night at the Opera* also reaches No.1.

Ivor Novello Award for "Killer Queen".

1976

May 29: Brian marries Christine Mullen.

June: "You're My Best Friend" reaches No.7 in the UK chart.

November: Release of "Somebody to Love", which peaks at No.2 in the UK chart.

December: Release of *A Day at the Races*, which tops the UK album chart.

Ivor Novello Award for "Bohemian Rhapsody".

1977

October: "We Are the Champions", backed by "We Will Rock You" reaches No.2 in the UK. Released as a double A-side in America, it makes No.4 on the *Billboard* Hot 100. Both songs are taken from *News of the World*, which peaks at No.4 in the UK, No.3 in America.

October: At the British Record Industry Britannia Centenary Awards – the inaugural year of the event that would become the BRITs, "Bohemian Rhapsody" ties with "A Whiter Shade of Pale" as Best Single of the past 25 years.

1978

October: Release of "Bicycle Race"/"Fat Bottomed Girls", which peaks at No.11 in the UK chart.

November: Release of *Jazz*, which rises to No.2 in the UK album chart.

1979

January: "Don't Stop Me Now" released, rising to No.9 in the UK charts.

October: "Crazy little Thing Called Love", featuring Freddie on rhythm guitar, gives Queen their first American chart-topper. It reaches No.2 in the UK.

October: Freddie performs with the Royal Ballet at London's Coliseum.

1980

June: Release of *The Game*, which reaches top spot on both sides of the Atlantic, Queen's first No.1 album in America.

August: The Deacon-penned "Another One Bites the Dust" tops the *Billboard* Hot 100, peaking at No.7 in the UK.

December: Release of *Flash Gordon* soundtrack album and single "Flash". Both make the Top 10 in the respective UK charts.

Freddie purchases Garden Lodge, a Georgian mansion in Kensington, London.

1981

February: Queen embark on their first tour of South America. They play to 131,000 in Sao Paulo's Morumbi Stadium, a then-record for a paying audience.

October: Release of "Under Pressure", a collaboration with David Bowie that gives Queen their second UK No.1.

November: Release of the *Greatest Hits* album, which tops the charts in a host of countries. It goes on to become the biggest-selling UK album of all time, with sales approaching the six million mark and rising.

American Music Award for "Another One Bites the Dust" (Favourite Pop/Rock Single).

1982

May: Disco-oriented *Hot Space* album reaches No.4 in the UK. It spawns the singles "Body Language, "Las Palabras de Amor" and "Back Chat", none of which make the UK Top 10.

July-September: Final tour of North America.

Contract with Elektra terminated. Queen later sign to US label Capitol Records.

The band members enter the *Guinness Book of Records* for their vast earnings as executives.

1983

October: With the band taking a year-long sabbatical to work on solo projects, Brian releases the mini-album *Star Fleet Project* and single "Star Fleet".

1984

January: Release of "Radio Ga Ga", which reaches UK No.2. This Roger Taylor-penned song marks a creative milestone as all four band members have now written a Top 10 hit.

March: *The Works* enters the UK chart at No.2. It spawns four Top 20 hits.

September: Release of "Love Kills", Freddie's first solo hit, which reaches No.10 in the UK.

October: Queen concerts in Sun City, South Africa, spark a backlash.

November: Release of Queen's fifth single of the year, "Thank God It's Christmas", which peaks at No.21 in the UK.

1985

January: Queen headline the Rock in Rio festival.

April: Release of *Mr Bad Guy*, Freddie's debut solo album, which reaches No.6 in the UK but fails to make the Top 100 in the US.

July 13: Queen give a show-stealing performance at Live Aid.

November: Release of "One Vision", which reaches No.7 in the UK.

1986

March: Release of the Roger Taylor-penned "A Kind of Magic", which hits No.3 in the UK.

April: London opening of the stage musical *Time*, for which Freddie records "In My Defence" and the show's title song. "Time" makes UK No.32.

June: Release of *A Kind of Magic*, soundtrack to the film *Highlander*. It tops the UK chart, Queen's fourth studio album to hit the No.1 spot.

9 August: The Magic tour ends at Knebworth, Queen's final live performance.

1987

March 7: Freddie's cover version of "The Great Pretender" enters the UK chart, peaking at No.4, his biggest solo success during his lifetime.

April: Queen receive the Ivor Novello award for Outstanding Contribution to British Music.

May 29: Freddie appears at the Ku Club, Ibiza, with Montserrat Caballé, a TV special celebrating the award of the 1992 Olympic Games to Barcelona.

October: Release of "Barcelona", which rises to No.8 in the UK chart.

Reissued to coincide with the 1992 Olympic Games, it reaches No.2.

1988

October 8: Freddie performs with Montserrat Caballé at La Nit festival in Barcelona. It will be his last live performance. The duo's *Barcelona* album is released the same month.

1989

May: "I Want It All", lead single from *The Miracle*, reaches No.3 in the UK chart. Four more singles culled from the album are released during the year, all making the UK Top 30. Queen's 13th studio album, *The Miracle* reaches top spot in the UK and several other countries.

December: Release of *At the Beeb*, a collection of recordings made in 1973 for the BBC.

1990

February 18: Queen receive a BRIT award for Outstanding Contribution to British Music.

Queen sign to Hollywood records, part of the Disney group, ending a seven-year American deal with Capitol.

1991

February: Release of *Innuendo*, Queen's 14th and final studio album released in Freddie's lifetime. It becomes their sixth UK No.1, spawning five singles, including the chart-topping title track.

October: Release of "The Show Must Go On", Queen's 40th and final single during Freddie's lifetime. *Greatest Hits II*, released the same month, will become one of the top ten best selling UK albums of all time.

November 23: Official confirmation that Freddie is suffering from AIDS.

November 24: Death of Freddie Mercury, aged 45.

December: *The Innuendo* track "These Are the Days of Our Lives" released as a double A-side with "Bohemian Rhapsody". It tops the Christmas chart in the UK.

1992

February 12: Queen win Best Single BRIT award for "These Are the Days of Our Lives". Freddie Mercury is the posthumous recipient of the Outstanding Contribution to British Music award.

April 20: Tribute concert for Freddie staged at Wembley Stadium. The Mercury Phoenix Trust is set up to distribute monies raised, which are used to promote AIDS awareness.

Ivor Novello Award for "These Are the Days of Our Lives".

1993

April: "Five Live EP", featuring Queen, George Michael and Lisa Stansfield, tops the UK chart.

August: Freddie's "Living on My Own", which featured on the 1985 *Mr Bad Guy* album, reaches No.1 in the UK, his first solo chart-topper.

Ivor Novello Award for "Living on My Own".

1995

November: Release of *Made in Heaven*, featuring the final crop of recordings made before Freddie's death. It hits No.1 in the UK and spawns five Top 20 singles.

1997

John Deacon makes his final appearance with Queen.

Ivor Novello Award for "Too Much Love Will Kill You".

2000

July: Queen's collaboration with boyband Five on "We Will Rock You" reaches No.1 in the UK, giving the band a chart-topping single in four successive decades, an unrivalled feat.

Brian marries actress Anita Dobson.

2001

Queen inducted into the Rock and Roll Hall of Fame.

2002

May 14: Premiere of stage musical *We Will Rock You* at London's Dominion Theatre.

Brian performs "God Save the Queen" on the roof of Buckingham Palace as part of the Golden Jubilee celebrations.

October: Queen star on Hollywood's Walk of Fame unveiled.

2003

June: All four band members jointly inducted into the Songwriters Hall of Fame.

2005

Former Free and Bad Company frontman Paul Rodgers joins Brian and Roger for the first of two major world tours.

December: Brian presented with a CBE award at Buckingham Palace.

2007

Brian submits his unfinished PhD thesis and is finally awarded his doctorate from Imperial College.

2011

January: Queen end a 40-year association with EMI by signing to Universal Music. New releases will appear on Universal subsidiary Island Records.

February: Stormtroopers in Stilettos exhibition opens in London, marking the 40th anniversary of the band's formation.

October: Queen receive the Hall of Fame honour at the Q Awards.

2012

July: Queen perform in several live shows with Adam Lambert.

August: Brian and Roger take part in the closing ceremony of the Olympic Games.

DISCOGRAPHY

Studio Albums

1973
Queen
Parlophone/Elektra

1974
Queen II
Parlophone/Elektra

Sheer Heart Attack
Parlophone/Elektra

1975
A Night at the Opera
Parlophone/Elektra

1976
A Day at the Races
Parlophone/Elektra

1977
News of the World
Parlophone/Elektra

1978
Jazz
Parlophone/Elektra

1980
The Game
Parlophone/Elektra

Flash Gordon
Parlophone/Elektra

1982
Hot Space
Parlophone/Elektra

1984
The Works
Capitol

1986
A Kind of Magic
Capitol

1989
The Miracle
Capitol

1991
Innuendo
Parlophone

1995
Made in Heaven
Parlophone

Live Albums

1979
Live Killers
RCA

1986
Live Magic
RCA

1989
At the Beeb
Sony Music

1992
Live at Wembley '86
Atlantic

2004
Queen on Fire – Live at the Bowl
Atlantic

2007
Queen Rock Montreal
Atlantic

Compilation Albums

1981
Greatest Hits
Atlantic

1991
Greatest Hits II
Atlantic

1992
Classic Queen
BMG

The 12" Collection
Atlantic

1997
The Best I
RCA

The Best II
RCA

Queen Rocks
Atlantic

1999
Greatest Hits III
Atlantic

2007
The A-Z of Queen, Volume 1
BMG Music Group

2009
Absolute Greatest
Atlantic

2011
Deep Cuts, Volume 1
TVA Film

Deep Cuts, Volume 2
TVA Film

Deep Cuts, Volume 3
TVA Film

Box Sets

1985
The Complete Works
Atlantic

1992
Box of Tricks
Atlantic

1994
Greatest Hits I & II
Atlantic

1995
Ultimate Queen
Atlantic

1998
The Crown Jewels
Atlantic

2000
The Platinum Collection:
Greatest Hits I,II & III
Atlantic

2008
The Singles Collection Volume I
Atlantic

2009
The Singles Collection Volume 2
Atlantic

2010
The Singles Collection Volume 3
Atlantic
The Singles Collection Volume 4
Atlantic

Singles

1973
Keep yourself Alive

1974
Liar
Seven Seas of Rhye
Killer Queen

1975
Now I'm Here
Lily of the Valley
Bohemian Rhapsody

1976
You're my Best Friend
Somebody to Love

1977
Tie your Mother Down
Good old Fashioned Lover Boy
Teo Torriatte (Let Us Cling
Together)
Long Away
We are the Champions/
We Will Rock You

1978
Spread your Wings
It's Late
Bicycle Race / Fat Bottomed Girls

1979
Don't Stop me now
Jealousy
Mustapha
Love of My Life
We Will Rock You (Live)
Crazy Little Thing Called Love

1980
Save Me
Play the Game
Another One Bites the Dust
Need your Loving Tonight
Flash

1981
Under Pressure

1982
Body Language
Las Palabras de Amor
(The Words of Love)
Calling All Girls
Staying Power
Back Chat

1984
Radio Gaga
I want to Break Free
It's a Hard Life
Hammer to Fall
Thank God it's Christmas

1985
One Vision

1986
A Kind of Magic
Princes of the Universe
Friends Will Be Friends
Pain is so Close to Pleasure
Who Wants to Live Forever
One Year of Love

1989
I Want it All
Breakthru
The Invisible Man
Scandal
The Miracle

1991
Innuendo
I'm Going Slightly Mad
Headlong
I Can't Live With You
The Show Must Go On
Ride the Wild Wind
Bohemian Rhapsody /
These Are The Days of Our Lives

1992
Who Wants to Live Forever /
Friends Will be Friends
We Will Rock You (Live) /
We are the Champions (Live)
We are the Champions /
We Will Rock You (Live) re-release

1995
Heaven for Everyone
A Winter's Tale

1996
I Was Born to Love You
Too Much Love Will Kill You
Let Me Live
You Don't Fool Me

1997
No-One but You (Only the Good
Die Young) /
Tie your Mother Down

1998
We are the Champions (re-release)

1999
Under Pressure (Rah Mix)

2000
Princes of the Universe (re-release)

2003
Another One Bites the Dust /
We Will Rock You (re-release)

2011
Stormtroopers in Stilettos